Rolan

Whirlwind of life
the story of Emilia Fogelklou

with much love
♡ Malin ♡

Emilia Fogelklou aged 45

Whirlwind of life
the story of Emilia Fogelklou

Malin Bergman Andrews
Translated from Swedish by the author

QUAKER *Q* BOOKS

First published in Swedish as:
Fogelklou, Emilia,
människan och gärningen
– En biografi

Published by Artos
© Artos Bokförlag 1999
© Malin Bergman Andrews 1999

This English language edition, translated by the author,
published March 2004 by Quaker Books
Friends House, Euston Road, LONDON NW1 2BJ

http://www.quaker.org.uk

All rights reserved. No part of this book may be reproduced
or transmitted in any form or by any means, electronic or
mechanical, including photocopy, without permission in
writing from Quaker Books.
Reviewers may quote brief passages.

© Malin Bergman Andrews 2004

ISBN 0 85245 354 X

Editor: Ros Morley
Designed & typeset by Jonathan Sargent
Text typeface: Arrus 10.5 / 14pt
Printed by Thanet Press Ltd

Photographer: Karl Hernried

Emilia in her seventies, cutting a dash

As soon as possible after the cease-fire in 1945 IAL (International work camps), which EF had helped to set up, organised relief work in war-stricken Germany. Emilia picks her way through the rubble of ruined houses in Hamburg, working practically round the clock, noting in her diary:

'Now I feel I've got work. All daylight hours are filled and [I feel] an almost constant inner joy, right through the thickening darkness out there... I walk in a whirlwind of life, and I reach out for more'.
(See p.168, with IAL in Hamburg)

DEDICATION

To all my friends in Sutton meeting
who have provided me with a 'greater family'
ever since I came to this country many years ago.

CONTENTS

I   EARLY YEARS (1878–1902) . . 1
Beginnings; Simrishamn – the home town; The windmill; A complex character; Grandmother; The task; Kristianstad; The Vanås Picture Gallery; Family; Royal Training College in Stockholm; In Gothenburg

II   REVELATION (1902–1909) . . 24
The Revelation of Reality; *Allvarsstunder*; Slättäng – and the debate on Religious Education; Romantic interlude; Hosea and Gomer – a prophet and his bride; Weininger; City of Learning; Philosophy; Fellow women students; Theology; *Frans av Assisi*; The Virgin Birth; 'University of Everyday Life'; Organic lines of thought

III   CHALLENGES (1909–1913) . . 56
Lecturing; Olaus Petri student in Britain; London; Paris; Italy; *Medan gräset gror* I & II; In Djursholm; Iceland

IV   A WRECKED WORLD (1914–1921) . . 74
The Hague; Sweden during the 1914–18 war; The year in Kristianstad; *Förkunnare*; Birkagården; Interruption; Kalmar; *Birgitta*; *Protestant och katolik*; The spiritual state of Sweden; *Från själens vägar*; Sickbeds

V   ARNOLD & EMILIA (1921–1929) . . 109
A late love; Arnold's story; Emilia on her travels; Meeting in Berlin; Arnold in Italy; The Fogelstad women; The cottage in the wood; Hard times; The child; Continuing; The new science; Friendships; Their daily bread; Lectures and other things; The year of crisis; *Kväkaren James Nayler*

VI   FORSAKEN (1929–1939) . . 145
America; *Den allra vanligaste människan*; The Society of Friends; *William Penn*; Illness; Women, awake!; Women's history; Academic adventure; Pendle Hill, summer 1939

VII   RENEWED ENDEAVOUR (1939–1972) . . 161
Germany, autumn 1939; At home in Sweden; *Bortom Birgitta*; Relief work; *Arnold*; Högfors; Pioneer again; Quaker ways; *Barhuvad*; Journey to classical countries; More writing; Ili ageing

APPENDICES
Chronology of her life, letters and select bibliography 186
Glossary of people, places and events 189
Notes 199
Index 204

1	Öland
2	Skåne
3	Malmö
4	Lund
5	Simrishamn
6	Kivik
7	Kristianstad
8	Gothenberg
9	Stockholm
10	Djursholm
11	Jakobsberg
12	Västerås
13	Högfors
14	Kalmar

ACKNOWLEDGEMENTS

For this English version of my biography of Emilia Fogelklou I wish to thank friends and family who have come to my rescue with good advice and language scrutiny, in particular Glenise Coxon, Elizabeth Page, Karin Petherick, Andrea Rivers and Eve Steel.
    I am indebted to the rest of my family and Jack for their undeviating support.
    Special thanks to Ros Morley, my editor, for her thoroughness and bright spirit.

The publishers gratefully acknowledge the support of the Anglo-Swedish Literary Foundation (Shaw Fund).

Tanner at work in Simrishamn.
Silhouette cut by Oscar Antonsson

I Early Years (1878–1902)

Beginnings

'The rhythm of her life had from the beginning taken sharp turns between humiliation and exaltation'. Barhuvad p 20

A little girl has climbed up on a garden gate facing an expanse of cornfields stretching to the horizon. It is high summer and the evening breeze is sending ripples through the ripe corn. In the lingering light of the Nordic long summer day the sky unfolds its panorama as the sun is setting. Evening after evening she comes to watch the colourful drama as the sun slowly drowns in an ocean of fields. She is spellbound, silent, deaf to all calls.

The child is Emilia Fogelklou, and she never forgot these evenings on the garden gate. In her later writing she regards this absorption into an experience as a most precious quality; to be able to immerse oneself into something greater than oneself is a prerequisite for inner recollection. When in her seventies she publishes *Form och strålning*, the introductory essay 'Perception' is based on these memories. She describes the scene with the girl on the garden gate, lost in wonder: 'was it an intimation of "boundless presence"? ... Did she spontaneously sense what scientists know: that there is an indestructible relationship between everything that exists?'[1]

Emilia Fogelklou was born 20th July 1878 in the quiet coastal town of Simrishamn in Skåne, the part of southern Sweden sometimes called its granary. She was the fifth child in a well respected family where her father Johan Fredrik Fogelklou was book-keeper in the town's only bank. Her mother Maria, though of peasant stock, had received an excellent private education and read several European languages.

In the summer of 1878 the newborn Emilia was greeted as a gift from God to the family. With her fair curls and her clear blue eyes the little girl soon had the world, i.e. the family, at her feet. The oldest girls were twins Sofia (Fej) and Johanna (Nan) of 6½; then came two brothers, Ernst and Hans Birger (Bie) who would be 5 and 4 respectively that autumn. After this flying start when four children had been born in three years, the family had had a respite of nearly four years before Emilia's arrival. It was quite natural that she was greeted with special loving attention, not least by the twins who competed for her favour.

In her autobiography *Barhuvad* Emilia speaks of her first years as 'a time of extraordinary splendour' with a glint of ironic humour. Amongst the innumerable little stories her mother told her the crowning glory was the occasion when she as an eleven-month-old baby was carried in to be shown off to some ladies at a coffee morning. The tiny Emilia determinedly dismissed offers of buns and biscuits, only to finally utter her first clear words: 'Best cake have!' And she got it, needless to say, amid general jubilation.

The incident not only illustrates the child's early ability in speaking, but her striking spirit to use it to effect, confident that life would meet all her wishes – a fêted little princess' absolute power in an apparent autocracy.

Suddenly the world was altered.

What tragic fate had overtaken the family? The answer is – nothing at all other than the 'happy event' of yet another baby. The ordinariness of this occurrence seems to mock its severe consequences: in Emilia's life it was a catastrophe. Conscious of the disproportion between cause and effect Emilia in *Barhuvad* self-mockingly speaks of her 'dethronement'.

It was one of life's cruel ironies that nobody had thought of explaining anything to Emilia about the little new-comer or preparing her in any way. People were not aware of the latent psychological problems in connection with a new baby in the family at that time.

Now it was someone else's turn to be admired and waited on; little Gert (from Gertrud) was now the pretty baby girl everybody doted on. An intruder had unexpectedly burst into Emilia's kingdom and usurped the power – and the glory. It was like the devastation of the garden of Eden. The passionate little girl experienced this loss with a despair that absorbed all her unreflective nature.

The crisis had all the classic symptoms of severe personality crisis: Emilia developed stomach trouble, lost her appetite and became fretful. Her curls straightened and lost their lustre and her family was baffled by her sudden outbursts of anger. She hid away like someone dispossessed, but would suddenly rush out from her hiding place, calling out: 'Love me, Mother!' only to disappear again to her lonely games with dolls that she pierced with pins or punished in some other way.

One is struck by the strength of the child's reaction and her way of working through it. This childhood crisis took years to ebb away. In the rippling back-eddy Emilia reflected on her destiny. It was the beginning of an analytical attitude to life. Looking back on her childhood Fogleklou observes in *Barhuvad* that puzzling over life and self-reflection became dominant traits far too early in her life. A little note-book carries her first entry in the seven-year-old child's large rounded letters:

> The bitterest woe of woes
> Is to remember in our wretchedness
> Old happy times

This piece from Dante's *Inferno*[2] she had found for herself amongst her parents' books. Seven years old, and so conscious of the loss of her childhood paradise that she blames herself for, as there seems no other explanation for her expulsion. With a smile at her own self-absorption at this time, Fogelklou describes herself as 'a strange little character, solidly built, with a round face and large questioning eyes ... who already gorged on her past glory.'³ This deep hurt would eventually be turned to positive account; an inquiring attitude is a spur to action: 'The path to oneself leads first deep into solitude, later on out into the life of the time.'⁴

Emilia's approach to life became dualistic: she would never again be able to take her place in life for granted; a lingering shadow of doubt of her own worth would always hover. But she was also endowed with a zest for life and a passionate temperament; a foundation of energy was thus pitted against deep shades of melancholy.

Simrishamn – the home town

'like a shell the Baltic wind blows into' Barhuvad p 25

Simrishamn was once a flourishing medieval fishing port with a large market place and church, but since declined. At the end of the nineteenth century it was an old-fashioned small backwater, surviving on trade, shipping and a leather industry where everything was still manufactured manually.

Simrishamn was a wonderful town for childhood. Emilia lived here until she was twelve and she loved every cobblestone. The family, now consisting of five adults and six children, lived in a large nine-room house with an ample garden just outside the town toll gates. Emilia's maternal grandmother, her father's unmarried sister and the housemaid lived with them. Next to the house was a windmill which became like a personal friend to the children. Everything was near at hand, no traffic disturbed the narrow winding streets with their half-timbered houses and large gardens. The children could play undisturbed, jumping and climbing walls and fences to play in each other's gardens. When Emilia was four and had taught herself to read, she begged to start school and walked the half mile down into town on her own.

The large tannery was a world of its own, busiest during the 'bark-season' when horse carts loaded sky-high with bark filled the whole yard, winding in a long queue from the tannery up to the market square with their annual delivery of oak bark. The cleansing but corrosive oak lye, an essential ingredient in the process of tanning hides, came to have a special meaning for Fogelklou and returns as an image in her books and letters.

The sea was another great fascination. Emilia specially loved stormy weather, the salt sea spray and the keen winds. She remembers the streets as 'dust free and windblown'. There was no pollution. Everybody helped each other at the two annual big washing days, when the sheets were laid out on the beach to dry and were 'pegged' by the clean sand.

The harbour was busy, wonderful to watch with ships being loaded with corn, fish and tanned hides, and others coming in with coal from England.

The windmill

'If you grew up with a windmill as nearest neighbour, you think of it as your friend.'
Barhuvad p 16

The windmill was fantastic for games and marvellous adventures. There was a constant traffic of farmers who came with their sacks of corn to be milled. The children were on friendly terms with the miller:

> There was a blissful world of possibilities. The miller's mate would hook you up on the chain and with or without a sack of flour you'd make the trip right to the top or down to the very bottom. Suspended horizontally you'd notice different effects of light and movement. There were fluttering fleeting

shadows on the floor, like strange swift birds, when the wings of the mill whisked past the tiny window. Everything that had been grey or brown and black or red was 'frosted' over with a soft layer of flour. And right in the corners were spiders' webs all powdered with white. Everything trembled, even in calm weather, when the chain-hoist slowly rattled up to the top or down to the mill base. Down there was black as night if the door to the road was closed. When the wings were thundering outside, you were enveloped in the creaking, rumbling and shaking all around. If it wasn't too stormy you could get a view from the balcony across the whole world: the undulating fields of Österlen, the ancient burial mounds, the farms, the flight of birds and the sea. But you couldn't find out the secrets of the wings from the balcony, for they were always on the other side. No, if you wanted to be near them, you had to press yourself tight to the outer wall of the mill, as close as you dared. There the huge rushing wings thundered like a hurricane. The fierce blast of air whipped and whirled right through your childish body, making it shiver with fear and delight.[5]

To live next door to a real mill gave Emilia a special position amongst her friends whom she entertained with the most fantastic adventures, flying into the night air, carried by the mill-wings. Until the day when one of the mothers, who happened to overhear, doused the storyteller with her disapproval: 'That's not true!' Disgrace and humiliation. From that moment Emilia forgot all her windmill stories. They never came back and she would never again be able to let her imagination swing free with the whirling wings and recapture her creative streak for the novels she hoped for many years to write.

Again she had reason to ponder on what was true and real in her own world and that of the grown-ups. There was no doubt about the practical purpose of the mill in the world reckoned to be 'real'. But she had also thought it was something more, a world full of strange secrets, sometimes softly playing as mill dust in the sunbeam, sometimes like thundering storm winds or the black-winged shadows of death. Did these realities not count? Why was this world not reckoned with? she asked herself.

This was a first confrontation between the mechanistic interpretation of the world and her animated world of ideas. To transmit a different type of reality, one 'that can change existence by allowing an *atmosphere* of a different sort, a radiance in the greyness of everyday'[6] later became a major part in her work.

A complex character

> *'From her happy first years, when everything had opened to the sun, she had gradually tied herself into a tangled and felted ball of yarn.'* Barhuvad p 24

If Emilia was over sensitive to correction by the adults, she was equally so to their thoughtless attentions. Emilia cannot have been an easy child to handle. She herself could often not control her strong reactions. When she stood next to her cute little sister who was petted by delighted ladies, and they then wanted to bestow a pat on the older one, she felt the condescending gesture to be a trespass upon her person and was on guard: 'Don't you touch me, or I'll SCREAM!'[7] And as an adult she never patted a child on the head.

Generally speaking Emilia found it difficult to come to terms with the grown-up world. She sought connections beneath the surface of appearances, her ear was tuned to the inaudible. She would hear what people thought more clearly than what they said. The answers she would give could seem precocious and a little impertinent – so she was corrected or ignored. Emilia felt herself misunderstood. She had difficulties in expressing herself – seeing everything at once, her words would not come out in an even stream, but rushed out by fits and starts 'like water out of a carafe when you hold it upside down', as Emilia used to describe her delivery when she got excited much later in life.

When father read stories, Emilia was absorbed. She so identified with the story that she unconsciously mimed all the actions that occurred. This made a comical impression, specially on her brothers who teased her mercilessly, until her mother intervened: 'Let her be! It's not her fault she has such a passionate heart.'[8] So the nick-name 'Passionate Heart' was added to her other childhood vexations.

Grandmother

> *'What Grandmother had meant to her in life was surely as decisive an influence as it was unfathomable'* Resfärdig p 67

If Emilia's world of imagination combined with her sensitivity to criticism often made her bump into the sharp corners of day to day life, there was a space where all such problems seemed suspended, where the very air was different and where she was always welcome. This was in the basement with grandmother Hanna, who sat in her rocking chair peacefully knitting. Hanna was blind, but exuded such serenity that the small Emilia felt sure that in her company she had an intimation of God's presence.

It was Hanna and her husband Per who had had the imagination and foresight to want the best education for their only surviving child. Per had been profoundly influenced by a religious revival movement in southern Sweden, remarkable for its piety and progressive attitudes. It was with the priests of this group that their daughter Maria received her education and she felt deeply indebted to them. All her life Maria retained her religious awareness and intellectual curiosity for all new and controversial ideas of the age.

Grandpa Per had died long before Emilia was born; it was grandmother Hanna who came to mean so much. But when Emilia was eight, Hanna fell ill and died. The little girl's world was shattered, she lost her sense of security and God disappeared for a while. She would never again be sure of finding him anywhere indoors, whether in church or chapel. But out in the great outdoors under the wide sky God was there for her again. Already then

Emilia intuitively saw her grandmother as a kind of ideal; later she became a model to emulate, e.g. in the essay 'The Human'.9 Unfortunately there is no portrait of this grandmother, but when Emilia visited the Panthéon during her stay in Paris in 1910 she seemed to see her grandmother's tall slender figure and gentle nature in the wall paintings of Ste Geneviève by Puvis de Chavannes.

Emilia loved playing in the wild part of the garden, preferably high up in one of the tall poplars, when the east wind blew from the sea and made both the tree and her body tremble with the blast. Here was a world she could steal away to with a book, far from her noisy brothers.

When her mother told her not to eat the grubby little currants given to her by the strange dwarf-like creature who came to do some weeding in the garden, Emilia was wild at the thought that Stina would not be allowed to *give*. And she ate them all, defying her mother. Then she realised that her solidarity with Stina had caused a rift in her loyalty to her mother – and so the boundary was created anyhow. 'Bridge building' became one of Fogelklou's closest concerns in later life, the closing of rifts between people, ideologies, institutions. Her parents' example guided her to a strong sense of justice. Mother had said that she didn't know a more upright person than Father. His marriage to a farmer's daughter was by contemporary society considered 'beneath him', an idea he totally rejected. Maria was his match in every way except in the social conventions of the day. Johan's appreciation of every person's equal worth was far ahead of his time, as was the democratic approach of her parents to life generally.

The extrovert part of Emilia enjoyed everything under the sun,

Study for the young Geneviève by Puvis de Chavannes (1824–1898) for the murals in the Panthéon, Paris

played the fool and joked with the farm hands, singing the latest hits and always on the go, while her introverted self was 'afraid of life', sensitive to all sounds and could not abide bad smells.

The task

'Perhaps she would write books one day. Or what?'

Barhuvad p 35

From her sunny and untroubled babyhood Emilia had developed into a personality of contrasts, a strange mixture of simmering life and extreme sensitivity, precocious intelligence and childishness, tossed between the joy of life and deep chasms of dark moods. In the tension between these poles something stirs within her, a strong creative urge. In a letter to a friend she many years later recalls a decisive occasion:

> I can remember myself as an 8-year-old. I had made myself at home in the attic, where I had turned an old double bed into a meditation (often crying) corner. There were also some books, I remember especially the poem "Om snillet", I knew it by heart: *"Do you feel your blood kindle, your heart beat* [at what leaves others cold] *then, O noble one, recognise the divine voice of genius, become great – and unhappy"*.[10] This was the 8-year-old's secret, nobody ever knew about it. But in that funny old empty bed I understood with incisive and clear awareness, as far as one can speak of such at that age, everything that was later to befall me.[11]

Thus Emilia experienced at an early age the initiation into a mission that she kept to herself, but which all the same implied being 'chosen'. It gave her a much needed confidence and a dimly perceived goal to strive for, though what shape that would take was still unknown.

Emilia's artistic inclination was partly inherited from her mother. Maria had herself had ambitions to write, but consigned her unpublished manuscript to the fire. Ideas of the time filtered through to this nook of the world through friends and acquaintances. Her father hardly had time to follow up his interests, but Emilia's mother stole time to read while knitting socks. Received ideas were debated, the dramas of Ibsen rocked the house and Nora of *A Doll's House* caused storms of discussion. But it was not until years later, when Emilia spent several months with her then 80-year-old mother, that she had time to get close to her in long conversations. Then she was amazed at how little she had understood of the crises going on around her as a child.

When her mother got Feuerbach's *Das Wesen des Christentums*[12] in her hands, she found the reading bewildering; the image of God as a loving father crumbled into nothingness in Feuerbach's radical interpretation of religion: our concept of God is only related to our needs. The belief in redemption and the sacraments is only religious materialism. Her mother's world was shattered, she felt herself alone in a void. But the responsibility was hers; alone she fought for a new foothold for her faith. When Emilia late in life was told about this solitary struggle, she saw it as a kind of spadework for her own striving – it was as if her mother had cleared the way for her.

An even harder time in Maria's life was caused by the writings of Malthus. She was then pregnant with their last child. There had been many children in the family and each one had up till then been greeted as a gift of providence. Now even this was questioned. Malthus claimed that great hardship in society was caused by the many children born, and in a time before contraception was generally available, he advocated sexual abstinence to limit population growth. It must have been a tremendous mental strain, apart from the considerable labour caused by a large family, also to be made to feel guilty for having brought the children into the world.

The last child – a boy – was stillborn after a long and difficult labour. Maria took a long time to recover physically and emotionally. In the end it was through reading that she was able to escape from her own problems and find her way back to life. This dark time, which must have overshadowed many months, occurred during the last years the family lived in Simrishamn without Emilia being aware of it. Perhaps it was Maria's need to recuperate that caused her to stay behind in the old home for several weeks after the move, hence not being at hand when Emilia so needed her during the early days in Kristianstad.

Kristianstad

'lost in an unfamiliar town and air and shy of strangers' Barhuvad p 30

The family moved to the dignified but stuffy county town in the summer of 1890, when Emilia was just twelve. It was the town where her father had grown up, but nobody was particularly enthusiastic about the move, certainly not Emilia. Her parents had decided on it mostly for practical reasons, as secondary schooling was not available in Simrishamn. Johan Fogelklou had been appointed district clerk which made it financially possible.

So they had had to leave the spacious house with attic, basement and garden for a town flat in a stone house facing other houses in a street. And the town itself was so different from Simrishamn as regards history and atmosphere: founded by the Danes (when this area was part of Denmark) as a fortification against the Swedes, it was built on the swampy marshlands of a river. The town was not and never had been beautiful, with a grid of straight streets and a strictly geometric town plan. All the same the little county town regarded itself as a cut above the other rural towns, with its District Court of Appeal and own garrison.

Here no pigs were allowed to forage for food. Here there was no view, no harbour, no sea, and the surrounding marshes caused autumn fogs and an air that often made Emilia feel giddy and slightly seasick. She never quite took to this town and missed the fresh saltiness of the sea; she felt ill at ease from the start.

Emilia and her younger sister Gert were doing their entrance test for the girls' school where they were to start in the autumn. Insecure in the new surroundings, Emilia did less well than her sunny younger sister. Despite the age gap there was only one class between them.

Emilia despaired notwithstanding that she was a year younger than the rest of the class. Study was her only preserve, her only kingdom painstakingly built from the ruins of the first destruction. Was this now also to be taken from her?

With Emilia the ground was well prepared for failure and defeat. Stiff with cramp and grief she lay in bed unable to move. Mother was not there and grandmother was dead. Emilia herself felt dead, like Jairus' daughter in the Bible. She, too, was twelve, but around her bier people were grieving and she was awakened from the dead. Nobody would come to wake Emilia. Father was so busy and the doctor he summoned did not know the family and had no understanding of the situation.

Eventually Emilia got enough life in her to be able to start school, a deeply serious little girl with a freckled snub nose and fair plait. By Christmas she was already moved up into the next form. Rehabilitation! But no, the damage was already done and irreversible, in Fogelklou's own words 'a deathly blow' to her self confidence. Her feelings of inferiority were etched deeper, reinforced by her early childhood experience, creating dark shadows of periodically recurring anguish and world-weariness for the rest of her days.

With the feeling of inferior worth came yet another inhibition. Since an early age, Emilia suffered from what she called her 'sin of omission': through mistrust of her own ability she did not act when she could – and later discovered that she had done wrong. She perceived this weakness as a form of cowardice, which she tried to balance by practising boldness. It became a lifelong struggle between whether to withdraw, escape responsibility or step forward, take part and say her piece. Her shyness dominated so far. Later it sometimes happened that she over-compensated for this tendency by a blunt directness – which she had cause to regret.

The school had a good reputation, with a full eight-year curriculum and a small state grant. The teaching in many girls' schools was unfortunately conservative and uninspired in both concept and method and this one did not entirely escape the typically wooden formalism of the time.

'Art' consisted of drawing plaster casts and copying patterns with coloured crayons. Difficult and boring! The only result was that after weeks of labour the rubber had worn a hole in the paper. And in handicraft you had to crochet a collar-bag with a fine white cotton thread that got grubbier as the weeks went by and the tangle grew; at the end of the year it still was not finished. During the rubbing out and the crocheting the concept of your own hands' incompetence was instilled, like a paralysing influence for years to come between the pupil and any practical initiative. Emilia herself never overcame the notion that she had 'shy hands'. But even such an impediment was not lost on her. Any painful experience was turned to a pedagogical vantage point in her later writing as she called for a more sensible and child-orientated education.

On the whole the years at school were happy ones. Emilia formed some lasting friendships. She did well; the teaching, especially in languages, was of a high standard. Particularly popular was the young teacher of French who had just come from the Ecole Normale in Paris and brought a breeze from the continent into her teaching. The girls were allowed to give talks, discuss freely, and express their own ideas in French essays. Emilia's imagination was fired by Romantic hero-worship and she wrote a rapturous essay on the topic '*Une heure de gloire vaut cent ans d'une vie*' (one hour's honour is worth a hundred years of life). Characters like Napoleon, and Brand (in Ibsen's drama), inspired her young heart, a mood that naturally was modified with the years and the two World Wars. What she in later years looked for was an everyday courage which found expression in everyday enterprise. 'Now there is no visible hero, the very word repels'.[13] As a pedagogue Fogelklou did, however, appreciate the heroic ideal as an aid both in religious instruction and general ethical education. She speaks of 'This valuable form for direct *identification* on the part of the child through imagination and feeling.'[14]

During a Scripture lesson the teacher talked about religious movements in seventeenth-century England, including the Quakers, who were, according to her, under the delusion that they could be guided by 'an inner light'. This was however something Emilia already recognised as being true, and forgetting her shyness she burst out: 'I have that delusion!'[15] – an interruption ignored by the teacher. Nobody would then have guessed that Emilia Fogelklou, after many years of research and searching, would become one of the founder members of the Swedish branch of the Society of Friends.

The Vanås Picture Gallery

'It was quite a new sort of reality she had met with. How infinite life can be!'
Barhuvad p 33

Emilia's ability to 'quite lose herself', in her words, was given a fresh and further dimension during the Easter vacation when her school friend invited her to stay at her home close to Vanås Manor, where her father was a bailiff. It was not the beautiful park with the swan lake or the great house itself that made such an overwhelming impression, but the collection of paintings there. The Count and Countess who then owned the Manor must have been away, for the two 14-year-olds had free access to the picture gallery where a treasure trove of some 70 works covered the walls. Even today the collection is the most important one in private ownership in Sweden. Here Dutch masters are hung close beside French and Italian masters – Teniers, Rembrandt, Chardin – this collection came as a revelation to Emilia. She had never seen such original oil-paintings. Day after day she visited them, lingered and allowed herself to be overtaken, flooded by them. The first night she couldn't sleep because of them. This interest in art became a lifelong preoccupation.

Emilia, age 14

Fogelklou came to devote a considerable part of her writing to it and saw in the experience of art one of the foremost sources for the life of the spirit. In 1954 she gave a series of lectures in Stockholm entitled 'Seeking in art, poetry and prayer' which made up the first essays in *Form och strålning*.

Works of art require a concentration that is similar to that of prayer. In order to be able to experience them 'we must remain open inwardly in a contemplation that in the end becomes a dialogue.'[16]

Emilia felt so at ease in the company of her friends at school that she forgot she was in fact a couple of years younger than them. When they were 16 and it was time for confirmation classes, Emilia was only 14 and considered too young by her parents. They suggested she should wait a couple of years. This turned out to be a mistake. Emilia was the only one in her class not to be confirmed. The old pain of being left out resurged. Emilia left school, unconfirmed but with excellent marks, not yet 16.

When at last the time came for her confirmation classes it was too late; Emilia found the young pastor a nice-looking nonentity. She already knew everything he was trying to teach her, had had time to become sceptical about certain parts of the creed and felt quite 'unworthy and unsuited' to receive the sacrament. But she did not want to cause her parents the grief of withdrawing at a time when confirmation was an axiom for the young. After many nights of sleepless anguish she at last found a place in the catechism where the definition of 'having faith' was 'with all one's heart to desire what these words promise'. This was adequate cover for her to be able to take communion and let herself be warmed by the old pastor's heartfelt 'may you be blessed for ever more'.[17]

Emilia's open approach to religion remained with her for life. The art of living that she recommends for constant practice is 'listening for initiatives in every situation, in continuously renewed seeking.'[18]

The family
> *'[Her parents] worked hard, with a zest for life and with humour.'* Barhuvad p 27

Emilia's open mind had been nourished by her home environment. She has warmly described the generous attitude of her parents. The children were allowed to bring friends home; play overlapped with homework. Mother would often help, sometimes with a laugh at some inconsistency in the text book. As the children grew they developed in different directions. There were all sorts of books covering the table in the corner room, reflecting the various interests in the family. Emilia's older sisters Nan and Fej were of a more orthodox faith than she – one was to marry the son of a vicar, the other wanted to be a missionary. Her oldest brother Ernst was a good Greek scholar and the younger Bie rather left-wing, his reading was Henry George's *Progress and Poverty*.[19]

The children were free to follow their leanings; the parents did not intervene. Caring, humorous, they watched over their children – with their share of troubles. Nan was 'saved' and evangelical, Fej suffered periodically from asthma and there is a hint that Bie's bohemian companions sometimes inclined to financial irregularities.

It's not clear at what point the decision was reached for Emilia to become a teacher – it seems to have made itself from her earliest years. At 16 she was too young to sit the entrance exam for the Teacher Training College in Stockholm, and therefore spent the intervening two years helping her father in his office and her mother in the household. Emilia with her simultaneously shy and impulsive temperament and strong theoretical interests was not naturally suited to household tasks. From school she also had a well established prejudice against her practical abilities; she succeeded better with her pen than with the pancakes.

Her mother would have liked to buy her girl some beautiful materials and fashionable clothes, but Emilia stubbornly preferred the simplest dresses with white collars, wool in winter, cotton in summer. No jewellery or other ornaments. Yet in unguarded moments one catches her relish for colours, a red winter hat or an embroidered collar. She never disapproved of other people's interest in fashion, it was only for herself that she cultivated her modesty and in no way wanted to enhance her femininity. She had made her choice, it was her mission (still shrouded in mist) – not marriage – that beckoned.

The Royal Training College in Stockholm
'three new, often happy schoolgirl years.' Barhuvad p 41

At last the summer of 1896 came when Emilia was 18 and could apply to the seminary in the capital where teachers for the higher girls' schools were trained. This College had been opened some thirty years earlier, inspired by Fredrika Bremer's passionate belief in higher education for women, for even in Emilia's time very few professions were open to 'the weaker sex'.

To her great surprise Emilia was one of the 24 students accepted that year. To begin with she felt awkward and ill at ease, a real country mouse, but she was not alone with her rural dialect – the students came from all corners of the country and soon she was walking arm in arm with some new-found friend in the covered walkway, as the custom was. A few years earlier Selma Lagerlöf had also walked there as a student teacher.

When her interest was roused, Emilia's eagerness dispelled her diffidence and she freely vented her views with peers and teachers alike. She was particularly interested in the philosophy of Boström, but when she heard the teacher presenting Boström's concept of God as 'reason' in contrast to our limited human understanding, she spoke her mind: '*If* God is love – why always drag in the old reason, as if it were a better part of a person than purified emotion, the translucent world of the spirit?'[20] The urgency of Emilia's question took her old teacher quite by surprise; it burst out as if her life depended on it. Emilia knew from her own experience that what inner help she had found at her most troubled times had little to do with reason. Had she not already at school found kinship with the Quakers' 'delusion' of believing in an inner light?

The question that Emilia so passionately raised was central to her life and would continue to preoccupy her for years – the testing of the world of the spirit against the blind faith in reason that dominated at the time. But the question had not yet been brought to a head; she was still just a teenager and there were still a few years until her decisive spiritual breakthrough one spring day in Gothenburg.

She left College with the highest grades in several subjects, ready to follow her path, but still saddled with poor self-confidence.

―――∞―――

Emilia happened to follow in Selma Lagerlöf's footsteps in taking up a post at the same school where her great contemporary had taught for ten years until she was sufficiently well-established to devote herself entirely to her writing. Emilia's job was to teach religious instruction, the Swedish language, history and geography in the lower classes; Church history and English was added in the higher classes. The headmistress, strict and skilled, watched over her school with an eagle eye, so that no new-fangled ideas were introduced into the teaching. But despite a conservative attitude she also recognised quality and soon came to appreciate Emilia who came in the autumn of 1899, inexperienced and with her 21 years, the youngest member of the staff.

So the old century imperceptibly slipped into the new one. Amongst the ideas that had a revolutionary effect was the Darwinian theory of evolution. Doubts about the historical accuracy of the Bible had been raised before – now they could no longer be swept under the carpet.

In the summer of 1900 Emilia was sent Harnack's newly published *Das Wesen des Christentums* by a friend who expected a shocked reaction to this clear account of a new approach to the Bible. But Emilia was not put off by the radicalism – in some way it seemed already familiar. The title of the book was not only the same as the work by Feuerbach that her mother had once struggled to come to terms with, but also its aim of thoroughly examining the whole premise of the Christian faith seemed familiar from her childhood home. She was stimulated rather than shattered – and her friend suggested Emilia for a post at a new pioneering school run on progressive lines. Gothenburg Co-educational High School was to open in the autumn of 1901.

Oh, how Emilia would have loved to go! It was like a call from a country she longed to explore: a new way of teaching!. She felt honoured – and declined the offer. For the post did also require her to take on the teaching of religious instruction, a subject in which 'she had so little insight and had so unprepared a heart'[21] that she felt that she could not undertake it.

But the school board repeated the offer. She felt she must accept.

In Gothenburg

'It is your task to create the spirit of this school together with the children.' (Artur Bendixson to his staff) Barhuvad p 46

Already in the spring of 1901 a small group of the new staff had gathered for a week's preparatory discussion. The headmaster of the new school was the brilliant young educator Artur Bendixson, friend of the famous Ellen Key.

Ellen Key, the controversial feminist, was seen as the figurehead of the new century regarding child education with her book *Barnets århundrade*,[22] which had brought her international renown. Here she recommends a co-educational model where the children would learn mutual respect and be able to freely develop their talents. A loving attitude would foster obedience and order without recourse to disciplinary methods. Such ideals were the foundation for the new school which was financed by progressive thinkers, businessmen, doctors and academics.

Ellen Key using her pen as a lance Söndags-Nisse 1900

The school manifesto as it was conceived during discussions, was that the teaching plan should be developed during the course of the work and that the teaching itself would be *'a part of the con-*

tribution to the time, a pulse in its very unrest, not presenting a form, but engendering life'.[23] How one should manage to teach according to such high ideals is hard to see. But all the young teachers were fired by Bendixson's enthusiasm, they warmed to his vision of the school as a living organism.

In order to prepare for her new job Emilia went on a course that summer, where she came across the writings of Walt Whitman and John Dewey. The poet and the pedagogue complemented each other in a strangely rewarding and very fresh way; Whitman in his visionary attitude to life, Dewey in his ability to put his ideas into practical effect. Dewey's *My Pedagogical Creed* (1897) describes an education that completely overturns the classical discipline – and here Ellen Key had found her inspiration. This summer reading raised a trembling resonance in Emilia: here there were the seeds of a teaching method that she had dimly glimpsed as a possibility – which if it could be made to work, would change the world! And Whitman as a 'caresser of life wherever flowing' was no less revolutionary. Emilia specially noted his high regard for women in her early essay 'On Walt Whitman' (dated 1901), included in *Medan gräset gror* (While the grass grows), a title which in itself reveals Whitman's influence.

Yes, Bendixson harboured great dreams for his school which was to turn Gothenburg into 'Sweden's spiritual capital' – and so the school started with the 'world's youngest staff' who had decorated the classrooms with birch leaves and Virginia creeper for the first day of term. And Bendixson tells a wide-eyed gathering of 31 pupils that it is *they* who are going to create the spirit of the school and that the teachers are there to help.

The eight teachers laboured and laughed, taught during the day and wrote their own teaching material on the cyclostyle at night. There was no separation between work and free time. Long before school visits became standard practice, classes were taken to see foundry and factory, they studied the cargo of ships in the harbour. They did bookbinding and brush-making; theory and practice went hand in hand. Emilia's life was brimming with duty to her task and devotion to the children; one of the most fulfilling times in her life.

Somehow several of the teachers also managed to find time for involvement in the fledgling workers' movement to the horror of Gothenburg's respectable citizens. The school magazine parodied the reaction and reported that Emilia had appeared as 'a rabble-rouser and that her fiery speeches had been greeted with the hoarse jubilation of the masses'.[24]

There were many outstanding intellectuals of the day who took an interest in the experimental education of this High School, amongst them Ellen Key. The famous lady had come to give a public lecture to a packed audience in Gothenburg which Emilia also attended, full of anticipation. But she was keenly disappointed and spent a sleepless night in silent argument with Key. When the great lady then visited the school the following morning, the meeting between her and Emilia was literally a collision, when they ran into each other in one of the school corridors. But Ellen Key warmly embraced her with a naturalness that took the edge off Emilia's stammered criticism. This first acquaintance would develop into a long and somewhat thorny friendship of many years.

The intrepid Key roused her contemporaries to debate ('one *should make a fuss*') to a degree that the peaceable Fogelklou never achieved and which she felt the lack of. Though sharing similar areas of interest, they had such a different approach. Fogelklou could never quite accept Key's glossing optimism in questions that to her had far deeper ramifications. On the other hand she never lost the sense of a secret link between herself and Key – in many ways her polar opposite.

The Austrian poet Rainer Maria Rilke, who also paid a visit, wrote an enthusiastic eulogy of the school in the Berlin magazine *Die Zukunft*[25] after a visit there. Emilia met Rilke who called her 'Fanfare' when he saw her coming with her skates in her red woollen hat. She describes the evening when he read a few of his poems – the gathered atmosphere of *'Der Schauende'* from *Buch der Bilder*: *'Wie ist das klein womit wir ringen. Was mit uns ringt – wie ist das gross'* (How little is that with which we wrestle. How big that which wrestles with us)[26] so overwhelmed her that she had to get out under the open sky to walk in the wind to calm herself. The words followed her all her life like the deep ringing of a bell.

bookplate from Ord & Bild, 1906

II Revelation (1902–1909)

The Revelation of Reality

'Maybe the deeper the predisposition towards melancholy one has carried within one, the greater the joy one is raised to at the transformation?' letter 28 Jan (1907?)

But beneath all the ardour and labour of life there lurked deep shadows in Emilia's personal situation as well as in the political one. Finland had for almost three centuries been part of Sweden – now as a Russian Grand Duchy it was suffering from the ruthless rule of the governor-general Bobrikov, whose aim was to reduce Finland's status to that of a Russian province. Sweden's sympathy for Finland was felt throughout the country; the Finnish theme also became part of the life of the school in poems and plays. How should one act before a superior force, with submission or rebellion? The problems facing humanity at large converged with Emilia's private ones.

Against her wish she had been allotted the teaching of Religious Education in the lower classes and some morning prayers. She did not feel threatened by the new scientific approach to the Bible and she was given complete freedom in her method of teaching. But the task of transmitting the most difficult thing of all – a religious attitude to life – was a responsibility so searing that it nearly destroyed her. How could she be honest in her teaching when she herself was struggling with the question of the objective reality of God? Did God exist beyond subjective conjecture?

The question burned in her mind. It concerned the whole

dignity and purpose of life, no less.

In this earnest questing she later felt that she fulfilled – or continued – a legacy of her grandparents' devoted faith and her mother's intellectual striving. The problem of faith devoured her, yet there was no friend that she could share this with.

Of all the staff, the headmaster was closest to her, in spite of their different stances. He was caring and supportive, at all times ready to advise and help. But at this time Bendixson was an inflexible atheist, bending to religious education as a compulsory subject: 'You know that you are necessary for the life of this school, but on this point there is a life-and-death struggle between us.'[1]

So when things fell apart for Emilia and she could no longer manage, she had nobody to turn to. In her despair she no longer wished to live. One cold and wet spring night she walked by the edge of deep water, close to taking her life. What stayed her at the crucial moment was the thought of the grief she would cause her parents.

During this time she felt she functioned mechanically, like a wound-up doll.

Then something happened that changed the world and gave her life a new direction. Emilia calls it her 'Revelation of Reality' which she reckons to be the most decisive experience in her whole life; this is her account in *Barhuvad*:

> But one bright day of spring – the 29th of May 1902 – when she sat preparing a lesson amongst the trees behind Föreningsgatan 6, there occurred quite silently, invisibly, the central event of her whole life. Without sight or sound of speech or human touch, she experienced in a state of exceptionally clear consciousness the great releasing inner wonder. It was as though the "empty shell" broke. All burden and anguish, the whole sense of unreality melted away. She felt living goodness, joy, light like an irradiatingly clear, uplifting, enfolding unquestionable reality from deep within. The first words that came to her – after

a long time – were: this is the great Mercy, this is God. Nothing is as real as this.[2]

The world was transformed – it lay before her glittering and fresh as on the morning of creation, everything in harmony with herself and her inner joy. Was this not to have 'life in oneself'? (John, 5:25) Within her was an infinite deep well of new thoughts, feelings and knowledge. The richness was too overwhelming for her to be able to fetch more than a few drops at the time.

Annunciation *by Fra Angelico (used on the front cover of* Befriaren 1925*)*

Her joy knew no bounds. Without priest, bell or psalter she had experienced how God finds a person and gives life, freedom and light. And she understood that what had happened to her was open to all people without exception.

She was so radiant with her inner glow that people thought she was in love. She smiled at them. Love for a single individual was not relevant – now that she felt carried by a love where there was room for everyone. This was the foundation for her conviction that everyone belongs together in 'God's depth', which she later developed into an all-embracing tolerance.

But a whole year passed before she could find words to communicate anything of what had happened to her.

All her life Emilia Fogelklou returns to this experience in different contexts. It carried her for months, years: 'During this time it was given to me to sense such a rich inner bliss, owning nothing, yet having everything, … it was just that bliss was there, not shut up in word-stores, but in the sky and the earth and the sea and everywhere.'[3]

She sometimes calls this experience her 'birth': from this she reckons her beginnings. She saw it as a religious experience of singular power, but never in dogmatic Christian terms. It started her on a path of seeking which eventually found its spiritual home in the Society of Friends.

From early on Emilia had taken a natural interest in others. Now this was coupled with an inner authority that came with her spiritual breakthrough. Much later she describes to a friend her consternation at this new self-confidence: 'I developed such a strange and strong self-assurance ... *this alarmed me exceedingly!*'[4]

People had already noticed Emilia's clear blue eyes when she was a child. Now they must have acquired that remarkable penetrating radiance that became the most striking feature of her person. Even turning to the camera her eyes seemed to glow.

She lived in this state of exaltation during the years when most others would find a partner to share life with. There were men who loved her during this time, but she was somehow beyond their reach. She had never been 'ugly', except to herself. Now she forgot that too.

But Odin, in Norse mythology, had had to sacrifice one eye in Mimer's well in order to acquire wisdom – maybe Emilia, too, sacrificed a vital part of herself in this well of her new wisdom, without realising it then? Her whole emotional life had been so absorbed in the inner experience that there was no room for other ties. Many years later she looks back on this time:

> I was but still a child,
> not even maid. And far from adult woman.
> Did not even understand that the flame scorched,
>   that it took my youth.
> I only felt for joy I was alive.[5]

Maybe this sacrifice was required, as with other women of note, for her to achieve what she did. Marriage, children and a home did not engulf her gifts. Now she just lived, radiant with the certainty that Reality, the revelation of God, waits for everyone.

With new-found interest she studied saints and mystics, to whom she now felt related. Now she saw their life and work afresh from her own experience. She felt herself to have been chosen like them. She spent the summer with her books and would row in the rickety rowing boat across to a small island where she read – or rather *lived* Jeremiah. Would she not also be called to a mission? How should she reach out to others with this 'new life'?

In the sceptical spirit of the time such things as a 'religious experience' were dismissed as illusion. Although she herself never doubted the truth of what she had met with, she felt she must put it to the scrutiny of theoretical science, philosophy and theology. It must stand the test of examination independently of her own convictions. And she knew she must be able to defend theoretically what she knew by intuition. She decided on university studies – she had to equip herself! Before her lay a long and laborious path of studies – besides her continued teaching she enrolled for courses in philosophy and sociology. Theology would have to wait and psychology she read on her own.

Allvarsstunder

'They have a genuine religious spirit.' N. Söderblom 1904

The new era inaugurated by Emilia's 'Revelation of Reality' also saw her first published work. She put together a collection of forty short pieces, little homilies from her teaching and morning prayers. They rose out of the ashes of the purgatorial flames she had just been rescued from by her inner experience. *Allvarsstunder* is the result of her religious teaching that had caused her so much anguish, the first work in what was to become a long search for an honest, down-to-earth teaching of religion. Contemporary material was either heavy, indigestible dogma or the dry crumbs of moralising. Fogelklou wanted to concoct a different sort of dish, more palatable for the young.

In *Allvarsstunder* she never leaves the child's conceptual world, whether she starts from a Bible quotation or describes some Biblical or historical person, linking text or story to something that the child would be familiar with. There is often a refreshing practicality in Fogelklou's choice of images. She humanises St Paul's exhortation always to be happy, by it being good to share one's joyful moments, but that when one is sad, it might sometimes be 'a good thing to be able to swallow one's tears'[6]. And of angels – who at the time were conceived of as white clad creatures with feathered wings – she says that they are difficult to describe, for 'one cannot see them with one's ordinary eyes'[7] and that they are as impossible to depict as music to be painted or colours to be heard.

The language in these little meditations is unaffected, there is no forced message or condescension – she speaks to the children as equals, a natural ease achieved by Fogelklou through drawing on her own experience – and as such presaging a modern approach to religious instruction.

But *Allvarsstunder* left hardly a trace, despite Professor Söderblom's favourable notice. Fogelklou's approach was too radical. Her work was largely ignored.

Slättäng – and the debate on Religious Education

'Christianity is in essence a mystical experience, a living reality for a human spirit, which therefore never can be imparted theoretically' Om religionsundervisningen, p 11

Emilia's teacher training did not suffice for entry to the university – she had to take the *Studentexamen* (University Entrance Exam). To catch up on her knowledge in maths and Latin, Emilia left her beloved school in Gothenburg after a couple of years and took a post as governess with a family residing at the Slättäng Manor near Lund on the Skåne plain. She could then study as well as earn her living. Her days were taken up with her duties, but at night she would steal out under the clear night sky of the plain and wander, open, receptive, listening, in a state of exuberance as strong as ever since her 'Revelation of Reality'. At such times she composed short prose pieces as a record of this state of being. Fortunately some were saved from oblivion by being included in a subsequent collection of essays, for example the vignette 'The Plain' in *Medan gräset gror I*.

Emilia had become known for her keen views on the teaching of religion and during her year at Slättäng she was invited to return to her old school as a guest speaker in the autumn of 1903 to deliver two lectures entitled 'On Religious Education'. The subject was overdue for reform. The Church held a tight grip on religious instruction which had to be strictly orthodox so as to implant the 'right' views into young minds. The method was learning by rote in forms more likely to stifle than stimulate any curiosity for learning in the children.

The teachers in the higher schools had not objected to this ossified approach. It was high time that a voice from this echelon of education was heard. Emilia was well aware that she was dealing with a controversial subject, but it was her passion for truth, not a desire to cause outrage, that inspired her to speak out. Here were questions that needed addressing.

It was not only a matter of method, but also of content. The Bible had earlier been considered as God's own word and every letter held to be true. After Darwin's torpedo under this ark, scholars had begun a critical examination of Biblical texts. The research into the historical veracity of the Bible was still fairly new and its shock effect had opened a gaping chasm between Christianity and Science. Nobody had as yet presented any practical solution as to how this crisis might be treated in school.

Today it seems preposterous that pupils were taught Darwin's Theory of Evolution at the same time as the traditional faith of the Bible, so that the teaching in one lesson was contradicted in the next. But at this time the conflict was unresolved. Most theologians kept their distance, afraid to take a stand in a matter that threatened the very foundations of their faith and teaching.

In her talks Emilia presented a solution with an observation that bridged the chasm in one lithe leap: 'If the letter no longer may kill anything, but the Spirit maketh everything live, then Faith and Knowledge can never come into opposition to each other, but it will rather be that Faith gives all Knowledge purpose and meaning, and all Knowledge can only confirm our Faith.'[8]

This holistic view was of course not new – mystics in all ages have borne witness to experiences in line with Blake's 'Everything that lives is holy'. Fogelklou here joins the tradition of thinkers who see a way to God in science as well as religion. But in the blinding light of the new science there was hardly anyone who was clear-sighted enough to put over this message. How could one communicate it to the young?

Fogelklou's answer is amazingly modern, both in its open attitude to religion and its democratic approach to the children: 'Religion is life. ... It is through the living contact between teacher and pupil that the religious influence is mutually transmitted.' The quality of this exchange depends on the inner maturity of the teacher, as s/he 'would not be able to communicate more religion than that which has become a life truth for her/him'.[9]

If the Bible can no longer be taught from a doctrinal point of view, there is nothing to stop one from studying it as 'a cultural document of the most immense value'.[10] The scruples of the conscientious teacher are also cleared: the subject can be treated like any other, without any need for a personal conviction. The independence and assurance that Fogelklou displays in the treatment of these questions testify to her inner authority, gained through her experience of Reality eighteen months earlier.

The Bible as 'a cultural document'! Religious education without any confessional teaching! This was inflammable stuff for the conservative authorities. And she did stand there as a beacon in her simple red woollen dress, burning with a conviction that must have lent colour to her cheeks and fire to her eyes. Afterwards when the controversy broke like stormy water over her head, her colleagues closed ranks around her like some young champion, but she herself felt no need for protection. She did not fight *against* anything, but felt 'nearer to the world she came from than the one she was speaking to,'[11] lifted by her inner awareness of a Reality where everybody has a place and all fences fall.

The talks were printed in the series *Skolan* which Bendixson published for the dissemination of new ideas. But nobody other than Söderblom took the trouble to comment. Anything that called customary practice into question was stifled by silence.

Romantic interlude

> *'Out of step ... When the rhythm of two spirits is so different, they meet at a certain point only to drift away to an incredible distance from each other'* diary undated

Emilia was planning to make straight for university in the autumn of 1904. Uppsala was the only university which included history of religion within a philosophical faculty.

But there was a deviation in her path of study. Emilia was not alone in having staggered under the burden of the high idealism the school subscribed to; the head was overworked and unable to continue his service. To ease the situation she was asked to return to her post for another year. She did not like to refuse. So Uppsala had to be put off, but Emilia Fogelklou made a start to her studies by combining her teaching with attending lectures in philosophy and sociology at Gothenburg university. She was equipping herself with intellectual armour – which however did not protect her against the arrows of the impish god Cupid. She later refers to this time as 'the Lönborg year'.

Sven Lönborg Drawing by B Chronander

He came to the school, Sven Lönborg, as provisional head, a man of integrity and excellent education in his early thirties. He had grown up in a poor but devout and cultured home, and his education had been paid for by a benefactor. Lönborg had already published widely on the history of Israel and other topics that reflected his religious interests. When he came to the school he had been a widower for two years. From his loneliness he was drawn to Emilia's luminous presence. She was seven years younger.

They shared many interests and they were both non-denominationally Christian. Jesus was a central figure in their lives, but they had no difficulty with the historical approach to the Bible; it inspired rather than impeded their faith. Both could be kindled with passion for a cause and be ready to work for it.

But there was also a difference in their approach. Lönborg took on the new criticism of the Bible with great energy and scholarship, attacking old prejudice and dogmas. But where he wished to liberate people from old constraints, clear the way and open a view to new horizons, Emilia Fogelklou did not have the same need. After her 'Revelation of Reality', logical reasoning about matters of faith had become quite irrelevant. The radiating power behind interpretations had become so much more important than 'views'. Sven's interest in religion was more based on theology, hers on mysticism. Emilia felt herself 'out of step' with Sven, at the very juncture where they had seemed to have so much in common, and unable to keep up with him or to take on his crusade, she withdrew. Their ways parted, but for years both cast lingering looks back.

Fogelklou's diary is very discreet. But there are passages that suggest that she had been the object of amused criticism for having jilted Sven, as this reported conversation indicates: 'Was she wrong to have left him, like people said? [adding]: "If you want someone more celestial, you'll soon fall foul of one of the Free-Church bible-bashers, you'll see!".'

Considering the strict taboos regarding love-making at that time, at least in the social class they belonged to, it is unlikely Sven and Emilia had an intimate sexual relationship – nonetheless it went very deep. Emilia felt she had been enriched by the friendship: her need to test her inner conviction against intellectual argument was etched deeper. There is no doubt that Emilia did love Sven. But she had to leave him to save her independence of spirit. The effect of this attachment left a trail of unfulfilled longing for years to come. All the same the decisive experience of the Gothenburg years was her spiritual breakthrough, her 'new birth' which also outstripped everything else that happened to her in later life. When she returned to the old school building years later, she felt the very air trembling round the old house where she had met with 'Reality'.

Hosea and Gomer – a prophet and his bride

'The higher Hosea stretched his arms towards heaven, the longer the shadows Gomer saw falling across the ground.... Hosea had forgotten she existed.' Medan gräset gror p 101

Summer of 1905 came. A respite from school, time to read, think and write; this time in the small fishing village of Kivik not far from Simrishamn. Here, her inspired reading of the Old Testament shed a new light on the story of the prophet Hosea and his runaway wife Gomer, a cryptic nut to crack – even for Biblical scholars. Emilia was fascinated by their fate – what was the human reality behind the brief account of the prophet Hosea and his silent bride who deserts him the very morning after the wedding night? In a flash of inspiration Fogelklou saw how it all could have happened and wrote their story in the form of 'Hosea and Gomer, A Biblical Fantasy' [12] in a night of passionate writing.

In the Biblical version Gomer doesn't speak at all and nobody takes her part. It is evident that her conduct is entirely irrational and reprehensible. Without transgressing the frame of the Biblical narrative Fogelklou conceives a psychologically credible background to Gomer's action. Hosea's many years of waiting for his chosen bride, the great difference in their age and Hosea's high hopes for his calling as a prophet become contributory factors. After the wedding ceremony Hosea becomes so filled with his spirit of prophecy, that he quite forgets the young bride by his side, has no time for her who inspired him. The fact that Gomer, neglected and ignored, leaves her newly wedded husband becomes quite understandable; the blame for the tragedy of this marriage which had hitherto entirely rested on Gomer, is now shared by both. This story, which according to scholars is thought to represent authentic people, has acquired human credibility for the first time in Swedish Bible interpretation. Here Fogelklou is far ahead of the feminist theology which developed particularly during the 1960s and 70s. Perhaps her 'Lönborg year' had deepened her insight into how a woman might feel in the close company of a man with a mission to proclaim? This summer she was to have still further reason to reflect on the nature of woman vs. man. The need to seek integrity and truth would incise itself even deeper into her consciousness at the cost of her artistic freedom of expression.

Weininger

'She was angry. But she read. Down to the last letter.'
Barhuvad p 61

From a school friend she had received a heavy tome of a book *Geschlecht und Charakter*[13] by Otto Weininger, which at this time caused quite a turmoil. With a splendid display of scholarship this 23-year-old Austrian expounded an unparalleled theory of woman's inferiority. She was declared to lack both logic and morals. As well as being incapable of any independent thinking, she was lewd and unclean. Any loftier spirit that could be found in a woman was nothing but a reflection of the male elements that she might contain. These very subjective statements were supported by a host of learned quotations and references which gave them an air of 'authenticity' and which made people take them seriously. Contempt for women was at the time as deeply ingrained as the teaching of original sin. A typical slogan of the time was that 'women lack a logical mind'. Very few understood that Weininger in his misogyny was mentally unbalanced and rather to be regarded as a tragic figure – he presents his arguments with the clearest logic. He committed suicide the same year as the publication of his book. A sign of the huge popularity of this work are its 25 editions in 20 years with translations into several languages. In this way it contributed considerably to the cultural climate of the age.

Emilia struggled all summer with the heavy reading, angry but engaged. For Weininger also said that 'one only becomes wholly oneself when one loves' and similar things she could agree with. Nobody could have read the tome more thoroughly. The 'Revelation of Reality' had left her with an inner conviction that implied commitment. In some way this led to Emilia identifying herself with all 'human sisters' and a duty to take on all that could be women's debt to men. At this time it did not occur to her to claim the counterpart: what debt men might owe to women. Rights should be given, not requested, in her view.

For her own part Emilia found the reading a personal trial, one more stone added to the burden of the feelings of incompetence from her childhood. She remembers it many years later 'so nightmarishly pressing' that she would have feared for her sanity, if it had not been for the well of spiritual richness deep within her. She worked her way through this onslaught with all her mental faculties engaged, experiencing her thinking process right into her very nerve ends, which made her identify both with Käthe Kollwitz' image of a thinking woman and Rodin's sculpture *The Thinker*. She, like they, 'thought with her whole body'.[14]

A modern reader might wonder at the degree of importance Weininger was accorded. But he underscored some of the cherished prejudice of the age, providing 'scientific' justification for current disparagement of women. Even at the universities he was taken more seriously than one would think he merited. John Landquist, a contemporary philosopher, represents Weininger's ideas in most respectful terms, and Strindberg wrote a tribute to Weininger at his death. But Ellen Key was not slow to denounce his ideas, comparing his misogyny to that of Strindberg and Nietzsche. In Britain he also received short shrift. The *TLS* briefly

Käthe Kollwitz, Nachdenkender Frau (Reflecting woman), Lithograph, 1920

reviews a translation of the 6th edition,[15] expressing the view that Weininger's picture of woman is unjust and unfounded slander.

This is a refreshing protest against the view commonly held in Europe, where a woman was constantly reminded of her inferiority both publicly and in private. As long as she kept to the roles determined by her sex, as wife, mother or whore, she was accepted in patriarchal society. But if any woman dared to seek individual distinction in some field, she immediately risked being pilloried. Any attempt made by a woman to raise herself out of her anonymity was regarded as poaching on men's unquestioned preserves. Professional women were therefore the target for sharp criticism, not only by men.

This same summer Fogelklou wrote an answer to Weininger's acrid attack in the essay 'A Conversation about Male and Female'[16] which takes the form of a dialogue between a brother and sister. Here Emilia applies what she has recommended elsewhere, which is to 'include people into our space even if they exclude us from theirs'.[17] We know from her diary and letters that she in no way wanted to reciprocate Weininger's aggressiveness; she rather tries to raise the whole discussion onto a different plane of objectivity and humorous tolerance in spite of feeling under attack.

Fogelklou had felt particularly struck by Weininger's accusation of *Verschmolzenheit* (inability to make distinctions), women's perception of the interrelatedness of everything, hence their inability to analyse and categorise. There is something of her own self defence in the sister Signe's answer: 'The word is uncomfortably expressive, I must admit. It strikes a weakness which is the reverse side of a strength, the feeling for connection with all living things, which is in the nature of women, for they know what life costs.'[18] We understand that Emilia Fogelklou particularly identifies with this holistic view and strives to see its positive charge. This is quite in the spirit of the great pioneer of the women's movement, Fredrika Bremer. She, like Ellen Key later on, saw that women had a special insight and contribution to make in society – something that went far beyond seeking equal status with men.

For local colour and personal comfort there were her kind-hearted and humorous hosts who entertained her with stories from Kivik, the fishing village. She gathered them in a thick blue exercise book where they were interspersed with her indignation over Weininger. So she managed to hold her own against him, live in several worlds at once and yet whole-heartedly in each one. But for many years to come she privately practised qualities that women, according to Weininger, were incapable of: solitude, independence and logical reasoning. It is a Scandinavian custom to take to the country in summer, and Emilia spent many a solitary summer vacation in fishing village or forest hut to pursue private research and to cultivate a cool objectivity.

The reading of the Old Testament prophets was a continued consolation for Emilia – she experienced them all as her spiritual brothers and in time was to devote a whole book to an imaginative re-interpretation of them. *Förkunnare* was published in 1915.

Truth she must seek, wherever it was to be found. This was her undeviating purpose.

During the autumn she continued this quest amongst various religious societies. She walked the streets of Stockholm, visiting the Salvation Army, Baptists, Methodists, Swedenborgians, Freethinkers and phrenologists, etc. She was curious to test her own experience of God against theirs, to see if it stood firm and if there were traces of it in other faiths than her own.

Soon she was to try it amongst professors.

City of Learning

'Has thinking not a narrower dimension than direct experience?'
Barhuvad p 77

Uppsala, at last! One day in January 1906, Emilia Fogelklou stepped off the train with all her luggage for the term. She already had a fair amount of experience in her baggage – six rich years of teaching, wide reading and an openness to the new ideas of the time which was to prove unusual in parochial Uppsala. She was 27, and in spite of a certain timidity, full of expectation and purpose. She had not come to find her way as a young student, but to find confirmation of something already attained, her ineffable 'Revelation of Reality' which had changed her life and made continued studies essential to her. In Gothenburg she had left a man who had loved her, perhaps still did, and with whom she had been deeply involved. But she had to give him up to seek her own truth. So far regret had not set in.

Perhaps she took a hansom cab through the peaceful streets to her student accommodation. Cars were rare and Uppsala's only tram-line (horse drawn) had opened the previous year – in another direction. Most student rooms were simply furnished with an iron bedstead, washstand and water to be fetched from the corridor. There was no electricity and the students were expected to supply their own paraffin for the lamps and wood, sold in sacks, for the stove. Mice were also lodgers – at times in disturbing numbers. When students wanted to congregate they took to the floor: 'Stayed on Tove's floor today' is not an unusual diary entry.

Uppsala was still at this time something of a rural idyll. The streets round the university were lined with old residential houses and large vegetable plots. The attic rooms, let to students, clustered round the university, castle and cathedral like bees round a hive. Not only the city, but to some degree also the different university departments had the air of a slumbering sanctuary.

Nathan Söderblom lecturing

In Uppsala the great breakthrough for 'the modern age' had come in the 1880s with the debating society of the student organisation *Verdandi*. Since then there had been a lull in the eager debate, but the years round the turn of the century had fanned fresh life into it, especially in the humanities with several names that went on to become legendary in Swedish university life.

Uppsala's languishing theology was vitalised when Nathan Söderblom took the chair in History of Religion in 1901. He had come straight from his post as Swedish pastor in Paris, where he also had received his doctorate in theology at the Sorbonne as the only foreigner that year. Inspired by the Socialist Evangelical movement, he had arranged a conference in Stockholm in 1897, where he stressed 'the duty of the Church to the new Workers' movement'. Söderblom was not inclined to kowtow to the conservative upper classes and the Church. Which exposed him to their criticism. With his liberal politics and openness to the re-interpretation of the Bible in the light of recent research, the charismatic Söderblom and a couple of his colleagues were still just sparks in a general theological darkness.

Philosophy

'Everything went with a burning interest, swiftly and lightly.'
Barhuvad p 68

But Emilia had long since found her own synthesis. Newly arrived at Uppsala, she notes: 'The deep divide between faith and knowledge, mysticism and rationality, will not be resolved until it is discovered that behind both is love, the wide deep unity in God that can "leave all free, as I have left all free".'[19] This reference to Whitman emphasises love as the foundation of life with its consequent attitude of tolerance. Even if such an outlook must be grounded in a personality, it can also be fostered by practice, according to Fogelklou.

There must have been something special in the air in Uppsala in the spring of 1906. Thaw came early. Already in March the gutters were dripping with melted ice and the river was breaking up. Emilia felt as frisky as a calf in fresh pastures.

There are glimpses of exuberant self-confidence in these first months at Uppsala, with certain reservations regarding the value of what was offered. She already knew from direct experience the limitations of scholarship: 'I know something better than knowledge, and that is the conviction which is one with the self.'[20] All the same, she was willing to undertake her studies for a degree in five subjects.

Already the previous autumn Emilia had visited Nathan Söderblom in Uppsala to discuss her course of study. She happened to arrive at his home the same evening that he kept open house for his students. One of these has left a sketch of the occasion, which affords a rare glimpse of how a contemporary saw Emilia at this time (included in *Barhuvad*):

> The professor's blue eyes in his lively face under blond, very wavy hair brushed back, were riveted with the greatest interest on the young woman who sat next to him and was telling a story, her voice and gestures immediately reflecting what she said – so spontaneously that Marit, quiet and shy, was almost shocked.
> – She is almost making a show of herself, Marit thought.
> But then she could also be very quiet and receptive. Her grey-blue eyes had such a strange expression, as if they were looking into another world, knew another world – huge, high, light above her – and as if she wanted to dwell in that world...[21]

Söderblom's seminars were inspiring – his history of religion included a wide field of literature. One series dealt with antique dramas and Emilia was allotted *Antigone*. This play came to have particular meaning for her. Antigone's fate in some way became her own: the unequivocal need to follow her own way, her inner conviction – ultimately based on love – even to the point of death. Emilia's reflection on Antigone's nature could apply to herself: 'Antigone rises above the others because she *feels* more richly, deeply, differently, and acts accordingly.'[22] Fogelklou's essay on the drama is included in *Medan gräset gror I*.

Another study that deeply impressed Emilia at this time was that of St Francis. Comparisons of medieval biographies had become topical since the discovery of *Speculum perfectionis*, a 14th century compilation on the life of St Francis, some of which is now regarded as a forgery while other parts seem based on authentic oral tradition from Brother Leo and other companions. St Francis had a special place for Fogelklou amongst the saints and mystics that interested her. The study of him, as of Antigone, became part of her own personal quest.

Philosophers and theologians do not usually see eye to eye; one has science without faith, the other faith without science. Philosophers have built on a tradition of reason since the days of empiricism; theology was founded on faith. Across this wall they glanced suspiciously at each other. But there were little cracks through which one could communicate. In the opinion of Hans Larsson, the gentle philosopher in Lund, the study of humanity should be a prime concern for the clergy. He therefore appreciated Söderblom's wide field of study which included classical literature as well as social concerns.

Emilia Fogelklou for her part wondered about Spinoza, the philosopher-mystic, who was said to have found his most important speculative revelations through philosophy. Was there no other way, 'some common denominator at the core of life that one could *discover* even without speculation?'[23] she asked herself against the background of her own mystical experience. Here Emilia Fogelklou touches on one of the main questions in philosophy through which she was to develop her independent ideas regarding the source of knowledge.

In Uppsala, Hägerström was the rising star in the faculty of philosophy. He had started as a transcendental philosopher but developed an ever more science-based thinking whereby any subjective experience was discounted. Philosophy had become science in Hägerström's definition of knowledge, which only allowed for the factual and definitive; other sources were rejected as 'subjective'. He had developed this view independently of contemporary European philosophy. The analytical Cambridge school, represented by GE Moore, Bertrand Russell et al., also developed their positivist ideas largely without reference to the rest of Europe. Yet there are striking similarities between theirs and Hägerström's. Philosophy's leaning towards science fostered a concept of knowledge limited to what could be directly observed or experienced. Metaphysics and intuition were out of the window.

Hägerström's positivist standpoint, according to which all

ethical considerations are subjective, based on sentiment rather than reason and therefore not to be accorded any value, was diametrically opposed to Fogelklou's: his nihilistic approach to spiritual values stands in stark contrast to her affirmative one. Was she rebellious? Dismissive? Crushed?

Not at all. Hägerstöm's logical precision stimulated her own thinking. His sharp intellect, his total conviction and dedication that won the devoted admiration of generations of students also captivated her. She found in Hägerström 'the best climbing frame' for her own intellectual development. Alone in her room she honed her arguments in silent debate with Hägerström, countering his emphasis on logic and reason with her intuitive system. She could not accept the one-sidedness of a theory only relying on the intellect. But she did not see herself in conflict with Hägerström any more than she regarded science as a threat to religion: parallel with logic runs the spiritual-organic, which to her always had a practical application – in order to prove a truth one has to *live* it, in all the dimensions of existence.

For the moment her greatest concern was to keep an open attitude to logic, 'dry thinking' as she called it, so as not to side with the opposing camp in dismissing what she did not understand. But with this open intellectual attitude also came a clear awareness of the relative value of learning. During this time in Uppsala, the citadel of study, she reflected on its superficiality – and long before psychoanalysis was known in Sweden she anticipates the importance of the psychoanalytical method, though she sees it in spiritual terms: 'Education in its general sense is a very thin culturally conditioned varnish over all the unconscious depths in a human soul. The most important element of all education would be *an illumination of just this subconscious emanation*, which philosophy gives no credit to and psychology never can disentangle. The means of such an education: meditation, prayer.'[24]

With her experience of mathematical discipline she felt there should be a correlation between logic and emotion: one should be able to purify one's emotional world, see one's own experiences, one's history from a more 'objective' perspective, in the same way as one simplifies an equation. How to achieve such clarity? She recognized from her own experience the need to work through difficulties by inner gathering, a seeking for clearness. The soul needs a discipline quite as stringent as that of a thought process or an athlete in physical training. Discovering that the word 'asceticism' originally meant 'gymnastics', she saw prayer as gymnastics for the soul, requiring time and practice.

Just as clearly as in the Gothenburg talks, she was aware that the walls between intellect, emotion and spirit must be brought down so that all capacities could combine in a renewal for humanity. But when she tried to impart this holistic vision there was no one who understood her, and she was dismissed as a woman who 'thinks into her emotions'. So she fell silent. In spite of her difficulty in making herself understood, her inner authority still commanded an aura. Many people sought her out for advice and to confide in her. She still felt rich from her 'Experience of Reality' five years earlier: 'One's religious metamorphosis transforms one's position in life: from being a beggar one becomes a benefactor, though wearing rags and lavishing gifts unseen.'[25]

Fellow women students
'They carried a kind of double burden...' Barhuvad p 82

At this time Uppsala university was a world of men. The few women students (then about seven per cent of the total) felt their presence was barely tolerated. They were excluded from the traditional student union parties and only invited to the balls as decorative dancing partners. Male superiority was taken for granted. The young women had to cultivate their confidence in order to make any impact whatever. In her diary Fogelklou notes some words about 'the ruthless faith in one's genius that is the self-preservation of the gifted'. It was natural for the women to stick together. Emilia had great resources for friendship and several women students became her life-long friends. Her first acquaintance in Uppsala was Dagny Thorvall, known as 'Tove', five years younger, a shy soul whose rare depth of spirit was lightly glossed by a girlish charm. The friendship that evolved was to become tremendously important to them both. They already had a lot in common – and in time were to have even more; both had a remarkable ability to be kindled by enthusiasm and wish to communicate the new ideas of the time to others.

Tove became Emilia's supporter and together they started a campaign in conservative and decorous Uppsala. They dared to give talks at the Christian Student union, Tove about Ellen Key and Emilia on Walt Whitman. That was a daring move! Key was the *enfant terrible* of the day, celebrated for her radical ideas abroad, ridiculed for them at home. In established eyes her ethics were considered as dubious as Whitman's eroticism – it took many years before his poetry with its mystical feeling for life, where sensuality takes a natural part, won recognition in Sweden.

The Student Union, where Fogelklou was to give many talks, meant a lot. But she hesitated a long time before deciding to join. It was the Christian element that put her off. She later explains in a letter to Tove: 'In my situation I should either join *both* the free-thinkers and the Christian Society or else neither'.[26] Tove soon left Uppsala after completing her studies, but she and Emilia kept in touch. Some years later they would be working together at Birkagården in the Stockholm slums and eventually cross the North Sea on the journey to apply for membership of the Religious Society of Friends (Quakers) at Friends House in London.

There were other young women students in whom Emilia found such empathy that they too became lifelong friends and members of the Society of Friends.

⎯⎯⎯§⎯⎯⎯

The first year of study ran smoothly and easily; Emilia took her *fil.kand.* exam (B.A.) of five subjects in a single year without a hint of stress. What made such an achievement possible was that she had prior knowledge in certain subjects, such as Swedish literature, and devoted less time to those. The exams were conducted orally and she had to turn up at eight in the morning for a grilling by the great Schück, Dean of Studies. With a light heart Emilia reports her results in a letter to Tove: 'First about the exam. Schück went best, although it was the worst. Because S was very angrrry and only gave me a pass, but I felt frank and free during the whole ordeal. And so you must understand that as I've always done exams so willy-nilly I'm happier to be able to be calm and cool when people are cross, than for getting top marks in aesthetics.'[27]

But if her heart was light, so was her purse. The two thousand crowns that she had received as a bursary from her Gothenburg school were almost used up, probably more through bounty than banqueting – Emilia was both warm-hearted and open-handed but lived modestly herself.

Now she had to plan her continued studies. Something in her rebelled. Her 'philosophical year' had gone with a dash, but the theology was daunting. To her diary she confesses that her 'wild-bird wings long to fly'.[28] She didn't want to be caged in by theology.

Woman under scrutiny, Tidevarvet 1927

Theology

'Mi was the only woman in the assembly' Barhuvad p 90

It was 'the men's knowledge' she now had to take on, single

woman amongst the budding priests, with a special permission to study, providing she made no claim to take office. She now must study the whole theoretical framework round the core of faith. Like climbing a rock-face, so she had to take a run at it. And she did. She found foothold in her studies, read Hebrew 'with all her might' and found it fun. Instead of its pale rendering in translation she found metaphors simmering with life: 'The earth was desert and void. And darkness was on Tiamat's face (The Babylonian dragon!) And Elohim's spirit brooded (like on the Phoenician world egg) over the water.'

So the Old Testament came alive with fresh meaning. Thirsty for beauty, hungry for knowledge she devoured lectures on Kierkegaard and Oscar Wilde as well as walking under the open sky in silent communion with nature. To Emilia the borders between nature and human vanished in the open, more through an intuitive identification with all living things than a pantheistic view. Snowflakes and forest acquire personalities of their own in waiting for the sun to appear on her wintry walk.

> Uppsala is still white with snow. Last Sunday I went for a long walk on my own. ... Suddenly through the sparse flakes appeared a fine golden glow at the very rising roundness of the softest snowdrift. Tiny patches of scattered sunlight trembled... and finally the sun itself appeared like a silent sermon for creation.[29]

Such little nature homilies with their lyrical concentration of a prose poem are far more typical of Fogelklou's diary entries than the robust realism of the practical world. So for instance does she never mention the great annual Winter Fair with its colourful elements of crowds of people from the whole of the north of Sweden which has been so vividly observed by several writers, here by Ture Nerman: 'hoards of drunk, half-tipsy and sober peasants roistered noisily through the town in all directions. On Vaksala market square the trading was brisk, ... the air reeked of curses and bad breath.'[30] At most Emilia's diary gives a fleeting reference to 'excursions on Shanks' pony and in sleighs'.[31]

Emilia made her contribution to the playfully serious tug-of-war between male and female at a student society. A visiting philosopher had given a hefty guest lecture on 'The Modern Spirit' – to which Emilia a few weeks later replied with a jolly parody 'The Modern Skirt' at a student party.

Social injustice contributed to the fact that religion held less sway while Church and clergy in many people's eyes stood for the conservative class-ridden and rotten society that had to go. But one movement in time often gets its counter-current. The beginning of the century also saw a succession of religious revivals in Sweden. The youth movements especially had a brief and abundant blossoming in the summers between 1905 and 1909, after which political events took over and they could not survive. The initiative to these meetings mostly came from private individuals and resulted in great summer gatherings for young people, as part of the national revival. 'The frozen earth is thawing and the great spring flood will soon follow' were the poet Karlfeldt's words to the students in a speech in 1906. Universal suffrage was being proposed within the government, heralding a new age.

Emilia, too, was drawn to the summer gatherings. In 1907 she was in Huskvarna at a large week-end gathering of several hundred Christian Students where a bishop lashed out at the young generation for its laxity and lack of interest in religious matters. Emilia mustered courage and stepped into the limelight to speak up for the students, opening with a question: 'Why should all Bibles be so black?', words that caught on and became the catch-phrase of the gathering.

In her defence of the young, Emilia Fogelklou tried to explain their predicament in that the orthodox Christianity they grew up with was something they now had to question. It was more important for them to discover their own individual way rather than follow a prescribed path. 'For when everything else in the world is uncertain, the only thing we can rely on is the truth we ourselves have discovered.'[32] This attitude of tolerance and emphasis on individual seeking is something we almost take for granted in our present climate. But then those simple words had a huge impact, creating a breathing space in the heavy atmosphere of Church authority. We can only guess at what rare power Emilia emanated on this occasion. The intensity of her own religious experience must have given authority and dignity to her words. The same thing is true for her as for other inspired visionaries, mystics, artists of all kinds – the atmosphere they created cannot be captured in retelling.

The same summer she settled to the task of writing the little book on St Francis. After a slow start, her work moved swiftly.

Frans av Assisi

'Who he was is difficult to capture in few words. A genius? But his intelligence lay in his heart.' Frans av Assisi p 7

When Fogelklou sat down to write the life of St Francis it was to fill a void. Paul Sabatier's great *Vie de S. François* [33] existed in Swedish translation, but Fogelklou aimed at something simpler and of much smaller format. With a light touch she paints the living St Francis without burdening the account with detailed biographical data. She peels off the epithet of 'saint' and calls him just 'Francis'. Already in *Allvarsstunder* she had described saints who had lived in humility and poverty, but who, since they had been canonised, had become objects of worship rather than examples to follow. She didn't want to put Francis on a pedestal of perfection, but make him accessible to all. Therefore she chose a small format and simple language that only brings out essentials. Fogelklou, like St Francis, saw in religion not so much a matter of creed as an attitude to life, in every domestic detail. In all his spirituality Francis was very down to earth and pragmatic in his caring, which Fogelklou particularly appreciated: religion as practical application, Francis with his ideal of poverty was 'perhaps after all a good political economist!'[34] Was he a genius? she asks. – No doubt, is the answer, but his intelligence was born out of love: he courts courtesy and joy along with poverty. 'Let those who keep with the devil hang their heads, but we should be joyful and give praise to our Lord', Fogelklou quotes him.

The fact that hordes of people left their home and fortune in order to follow Francis in a life of poverty was essentially through his personal magnetism, the power emanating from the fact that 'he was *alive to his utmost ability*'.35

Frans av Assisi was intended for laymen and teachers. It has been reprinted several times, still current in its simplicity, like a small posy of wayside flowers handed to a passing traveller.

Between periods of study and writing, Fogelklou's family home was a welcome refuge. The interchange between Emilia and her parents was warm and mutual. But a troubled period began when both her older sister Fej and her father were diagnosed with cancer. Emilia visited them both in hospital. Her father was soon home again, but her sister was weaker. It would take years of nursing before they died, 1915 and 1921 respectively. Emilia Fogelklou's studies also took a difficult turn.

The Virgin Birth

> '***Honesty, purity** and **faithfulness**! Help me! Scour me with lye if you so wish, and may it hurt! But keep me pure, pure and steadfast.*'   diary 16.10.1907

This passionate plea was met in full measure. A couple of months later she mutters: 'I was given all the "lye" and more than I requested, was well and truly tanned'.36 The lye she had been laundered in was the seminar of the Virgin Birth. The course was compulsory, she could not avoid sitting there, alone amongst the men, while the orthodox teaching of a miraculous conception proceeded inexorably week after week. There seemed to be no room for a more subtle metaphorical explication and Emilia began to feel desperately confined. This locked and literal interpretation of the old dogmas threatened to crumble her sense of Jesus as a living person, his humanity and historical connection with the old prophets.

Emilia, who always reacted with physical symptoms to psychic states, felt sickened. Her despair increased as the seminar ground on, so did her nausea, until she had to be rushed to hospital one day with a ruptured appendix. This serious illness released her from the course – and also nearly from life itself. But she did survive, and later wondered to herself if her illness was not a striking metaphor – she had literally been unable to digest an orthodox dogma she could not accept.

How different this year was to her last one, when study had been so stimulating! During the weeks of convalescence she reflected on her youth which seemed dead and gone. Marriage and children had evidently not come her way. And she had not been allowed to die. 'What will then be my work, as I did not slip through the door to the next world, which I so eagerly desired?'[37] At this and many other times in her life, death would have come as a welcome relief.

It took her a while to gather herself and find new strength. Which she did. Did 'oodles of proofreading' and got out for walks in the woods as soon as her legs would carry her.

But she had lost a sense of direction. And was close to giving up her theological studies – but were they not to have served a purpose?

> A great beauty met me, showed me God's marvel.
> And then it disappeared from my world,
> Leaving me with an immense responsibility.
>
> Dusk is falling, chill descends
> I'm weary, I'm alone.
> Faith is feeble and more so I.
> Did 'God's fighter' turn poltroon?[38]

Her 'Revelation of Reality' had implied a calling, promised a path. She still waited for inner guidance to know her direction. While she dutifully laboured in her academic harness, her patience sometimes ran out: 'I'm hungry and thirsty for people-work. All this study seems a strangely extended preparation. Give me a proper job, soon!!'[39]

Children had a central role in the 'people-work' Fogelklou so eagerly desired. Their spiritual fostering was her prime interest in the seminars on the teaching of religion in schools. Her attitude was as radical as ever; she wanted to write books with no reference to creed, freely from her own inspiration, capturing the children's interest by a glimpse of her own vision, for: 'works of art cannot be forced upon anyone; even less religion.'[40] Yet writing seemed to her a very inadequate means of expression compared with life. 'A brilliant thought is impressive, a wonderful poem even more so, perhaps. But to really live in the moment of the day directly, truthfully, from the depths, not merely by instinct or habit, would mean so much more.... Artist? Preacher? Me! No, *human*. That is all I ask.'[41] She came to set her involvement in life before all else and never considered herself to be other than 'the most ordinary human creature'.

'University of Everyday Life'

> *'I feel like a wild-brain who has taken up residence in the skull of the most obliging sheep that's grazed God's earth.'*
> diary 29.12.1908

The sheep wanted to follow the flock, submit to the law of the group, be 'the most ordinary' of all – her wild-brain demanded independence, wanted to break out of every conventional phrase, thought, situation.

Emilia got plenty of practice for her human role at her visits home, where there was Titten, her godson, to coax medicine into, when all other members of the family failed to do so. And the old family doctor who with all his professional authority denounced Emilia Fogelklou for her studies – for it was women's task to care for others and relieve the desperate need of the destitute. Questions of universal suffrage and women's right to study were inessential in a wretched world. Emilia had to ransack her conscience for justification, questioning the value of her work.

The traditional Christmas festivities could also be a trial: 'Party at our home. I think that "excellent" people are the most unbearable around. Myself I'm unbearable today without being the slightest bit excellent.'[42] In the 'wrong' company Emilia didn't come into her own, on the contrary she felt she had 'those horrible mephisto-eyes that see small black creepy-crawlies everywhere...'[43]

But only a few days later Emilia was called to a friend's sickbed. Gerda, her friend from school was suffering from a heart condition. Emilia, who had been on her way to the dentist, cancelled her appointment and went to Gerda. The hours gently passed as she cradled her sick friend in her arms while reading to her. Gerda died so quietly that Emilia was not quite aware of it happening. Only later at night her nerves transmitted the sense of the gradual cooling and stiffening of the body in her embrace. It was Emilia's first close encounter with death, profound, but in no way frightening. 'Brother Death' as she liked to call him in a Franciscan spirit, was to become very familiar through all the death-beds she came to sit by.

Though Emilia had to fund her own studies, she still felt her position as a student to be a privilege. Her 'social conscience' would not leave her alone. From all corners urgent voices called her and louder than any was the situation of industrial workers. Their wages were still not regulated, the gulf between rich and poor still gaped as wide as ever. The poor had no right to vote and no means of championing their own cause.

Later in the summer of 1909 came the Great Strike, affecting the whole country, the workers' response to the employers' attempt to lower their wages even further. The strike was intended as a lightning war, it was countrywide and almost half the workforce downed tools. But as employers had unsold stock and the railway still functioned the situation developed into an extended war of starvation. When union strike-funds ran out after a few weeks, the strike had to be called off. The workers were forced to return to work on even lower wages.

News of the strike reached Emilia Fogelklou and her friend who spent the summer studying in a small fishing village. It seemed oddly ironical to Emilia that she with her longing for practical 'people-work' was unable to take part, but must study the history of dogmas for the last lap of her degree. Her social involvement must wait.

Now the first thing was to finish. On September 15th she noted two words in her diary: 'teol.kand', B.D., Bachelor of Divinity – she was the first woman in Sweden with this degree and many years ahead of British women who were only admitted to this qualification in the 1930s. Completing her studies was mere formality to Emilia, and having got this out of the way, she devoted her last days in Uppsala to passionate work trying to formulate something that had matured during her years of study – her so called 'organic line'. Söderblom was so fascinated by these thoughts that he asked her to return in December to present them at his end of term seminar in the philosophy of religion.

Organic lines of thought

> *'She herself considered emotive and aesthetic insight to have a special place in religious awareness.'* Barhuvad p 111

The autumn passed in eager work at home in Kristianstad, until Fogelklou's 'organic thesis' took shape, given the modest title 'Attempts at understanding'. In practical terms this was the first systematic criticism of purely logical thinking as defined by Hägerström. Here she confronts the opposites of logical thinking and intuitive insight. With a kind of humorous acumen she shows the absurdity of only relying on logic: pure reasoning can 'disprove' the existence of God with very similar arguments used to 'prove' it. While not denying the merits of logic, she points out that intuitive, spiritual experience is of equal importance for human understanding. 'Attempts at understanding' was included in her first collection of essays, *Medan gräset gror* (1911).

The seminar continued for several hours, followed by a very lively discussion, but Fogelklou's ideas were run into the ground. Nobody had dared to express sympathy for her line of thought. Many years later she heard that at least two students at the time had found her work liberating, 'but one was too ashamed to admit one's appreciation of 'women's philosophy' in front of the others.'

Emilia felt her work was wasted and that she had failed in her aim of reaching out to people. God didn't need her work. She was the one who had to learn from others. Not in the passive sense of 'understanding is forgiving', but in an active kind of identification with the other person. This lithe tolerance rose within her like a steel spring out of the sense of defeat, and in spite of the family doctor's disapproval, which still nagged her mind – perhaps he had been right after all about the uselessness of her studies.

She was not heard and not understood – ahead of her time.

III Challenges (1909–1913)

Lecturing

'It was a comical thing to represent Dr Keijser'
Barhuvad p 121

Emilia's first task was to organise her life. Her studies had left debts and she had to find a job. She had the honour of being offered a temporary post as lecturer in religion, replacing old Dr. Keijser, at the College where she herself had trained as a teacher. In spite of having looked forward to this post, she found it alien to her nature: 'I haven't got that gliding dignity that one expects from a lecturer. Nobody has ragged me – I'm wandering around like a harmless and obliging dolt – but I am in such a foreign country, Tove.' She was choking in the institutional atmosphere – 'I just gasp for *air, air, air!!*'[1] But she struggled on, and with her usual energy also found time for museum visits, exhibitions, the popular religious discussions at the 'People's Palace' ('I like the audience a lot, but rarely the speakers') and excursions with the group of women factory workers that Ellen Key had initiated, where Fogelklou made some important and lasting friendships.

Her energies were called upon in all kinds of human situations, whether to edit and publish some friend's posthumous work or rush to the sickbed of another. The fate of several women, whom she had known as students in Uppsala, touched her to the quick. Fogelklou felt that they had foundered in the steely structure of a male-dominated society. Greta Beckius was one whom she tried to help, but Greta had been damaged beyond repair by a love-affair that was to cost her her life. The man was casual, she had wagered all. She had tried to come to terms with this wrecked love by writing it into a novel. Before she took her life with a revolver, she entrusted the manuscript to Emilia who was devastated by Greta's suicide as well as by her novel, which was the most painful reading she had ever experienced.

Outwardly, Fogelklou was the strong supportive rock for all to lean on, but privately she suffered a long low period. An added factor was probably her inability to find a job. All positions she applied for came to nothing, maybe she was one of the first to be overqualified and superfluous? There seemed no purpose for her to fulfil.

But one day in the spring of 1910 the world opened before her. Someone had spotted Fogelklou's potential and the post brought a letter from the Olaus Petri Society, which annually gave one bursary, with an offer to travel for the study of 'present-day religious and philosophical movements' in Europe for a year – England, France, Italy. Excitedly Emilia started learning Italian in preparation for the journey – she was already fluent in English, French and German.

As a sort of baptism by fire she attended the large ecclesiastical Örebro meeting which took place in the summer of 1910 before her departure. It was the great confrontation between the teaching of the Church and modern science, the purpose of which was to establish the basis for Christianity in relation to the new scientific discoveries. People were leaving the Church in droves, despite all the efforts made in preaching and the teaching of religion. What had gone wrong? The debate was heated, but often the two sides did not really listen to each other.

To Fogelklou's mind the real conflict was between personal conviction and official creed. She felt that in all the pomp and circumstance of the Church with its rituals and ceremonies, the living expression of a personal faith seemed lost. Fogelklou was one of the speakers on the teaching of religion. Her stress on the importance of a genuine and simple approach was ridiculed by the church press.

That summer Fogelklou wrote her own version of a beatitude: 'Blessed are those that never give up the struggle for the one living Truth.' Was it her own task she had in mind?[2]

Olaus Petri student in Britain
The countryside

At the beginning of August 1910 Emilia Fogelklou left Copenhagen on a steamer bound for Newcastle upon Tyne on her first journey abroad. The first stop was Hull where they arrived one Sunday morning for loading and unloading. Emilia listened fascinated to the peal of church bells that reached her across the water, so much lighter and more playful than the weighty monotone of Swedish bells. She reflected on the difference in religious life between the two countries. Historically, religious interest had much firmer roots in Britain, she felt, and now she would be able to study it in the present day. Her visit began with a stay with her sister Nan and Nan's husband Alfred Wancke in their Hexham home.

They came to meet her in Newcastle with horse and trap. The sisters had a welcome opportunity to meet and Emilia to get familiar with colloquial English. Nan was not in the same seeking phase as Emilia; she and her husband belonged to the Plymouth Brethren, where Emilia found much that pleased her, especially the element of silent worship. But men and women were separated and women were not allowed to speak in the congregation. To Emilia Fogelklou's mind, however, it was the men, not the women who were the greater losers: 'I always pity the "Plymouth men" because they must be tempted to despotism with such a dogma as backbone.'[3]

All expressions of religious seeking were of interest to Emilia. Four years earlier she had spent an autumn in Stockholm visiting different religious groups in a kind of spontaneous ecumenism and here she resumed the quest amongst all the different religious sects of the area. She found amongst these genuinely pious people a great generosity towards the less fortunate in society, but hardly any desire for social reform. The calm conservatism of Britain had not yet been shattered by a World War, and the Empire was still largely unchallenged.

London

The contrast Emilia experienced on arrival in London at the end of

September could hardly have been greater. She fell straight into one of the most difficult crises the Catholic church had seen. The conflict was between the liberal movement, modernism, which sought to reform the church from within, and the reactionary Pope Pius X. The modernists represented the best element in the young generation of devoted work and idealism – while the Pope unfortunately was pious and limited, afraid the Catholic faith would be corrupted by heresy. The latest strike against the modernists was the papal ban on the French organisation *Le Sillon* (The Furrow) and its activities to ease the lot of the proletariat: clubs, crêches, discussion groups, etc. Was all this work really to cease?

A Daniel in this situation was Friedrich von Hügel, a friend of Nathan Söderblom from his time in Paris, and the first person Emilia looked up in London. Nobody could have received her with greater kindness and warmth than this 'arch-modernist' out of reach of the long arm of the Pope, as von Hügel was a Catholic but not a priest. He clearly saw that the entrenchment of the Pope and his associates behind a narrow orthodoxy was quite untenable, and that the Catholic 'universal' church had become its own paradox. But he also affirmed that there is much that one has to submit to in life, that the relationship between an individual and society demands much compromise and sacrifice in order to serve the whole, and that it is right that it should be so. 'Life at its best is an expensive thing, a most expensive thing' were words that Emilia never forgot. In von Hügel she found the most profound expression of the Catholic faith; their correspondence of many years is unfortunately lost, but Fogelklou has saved some important letters by including them in her essay on him.[4]

Von Hügel assisted Emilia in every way. He lent or gave her books, helped her make up a whole programme of study for her time in London and introduced her to the Quakers. His name functioned as a magic 'sesame': doors opened to clubs, libraries, meetings where she would otherwise not have access.

In London Emilia stayed at a small guest house in Herne Hill and during the autumn became familiar with coal fires, hot water bottles and suffragette action. The first two had a certain relaxed

English charm; the latter was disturbing. In the face of persistent refusal by Parliament to discuss women's suffrage, the atmosphere had become very tense, leading up to the 'Black Friday' of 18 November, when a deputation of women were obstructed by the police and a riot broke out by the House of Commons, ending with the arrest of 120 women. By this time Emilia was already in France, but she had seen earlier evidence of the struggle: 'the riots are terrible to my mind', she notes in her October diary. For her the only way to achieve any goal was through peaceful means, not militancy.

London was a city of stark contrasts with its three million inhabitants and glaring social injustice. In some areas people lived in luxury while the destitution in others was unimaginable. Yet this was the city where Marx and Engels had agitated and Marx had written *Das Kapital* a couple of decades earlier. Fogelklou watched and wondered.

Without Emilia knowing it, a similar idea was already germinating in the minds of a couple of Swedish pioneers, Natanael Beskow and Ebba Pauli, which soon bore fruit in Birkagården, the settlement in Stockholm where she was to become an energetic and supportive worker.

Paris

'Beautiful, kind, homely Britain, farewell!' is Fogelklou's first diary entry in Paris, October 1910, where she encountered a totally different reality in the dingy boarding house where she was shown into a grubby dark room by 'a little grey-black madame with grey-black lace on her thin grey hair and a couple of grey-black teeth in her tired mouth.'

Out in the streets she watched a large cab driver act like a bear in play with a small child; people joked, quarrelled, hugged each other with a spontaneity she never saw in London streets. Emilia soon realised that the French understood *amour* and art so much better than elsewhere. Soon she writes 'Beautiful, delightful Paris that gives a sense of Art and strikes fresh chords.'[5] Emilia's emotional response was roused, and when she was allowed to hold madame's new great-grandchild in her arms, she felt a brooding longing for a child like never before. She was 32 and thought that marriage and children had passed her by.

Paris in 1910 was the great magnetic metropole for artists. Gertrude Stein was in town, visiting Picasso's new studio at rue Ravignan where he was exploring cubism together with Braque. Chagall, who this year had arrived from Vitebsk found fresh inspiration in cubism which he transformed into lyric symbolism, which inspired Apollinaire to coin the word 'surnaturel', which later became 'surréel'; and 'surrealism' was established.

Even if Emilia did not have any direct contact with bohemian life and the artistic avantgarde, she experienced the atmosphere intuitively: 'I sleep so much worse here than in England, but I live more.'[6] Rodin was at the height of his fame. Emilia passed his *Penseur* (The Thinker) almost every day and felt identified with his physical concentration in which she found even 'every vertebra thinking'.[7]

Every morning she spent some hours at the Louvre, often stopping before Nike of Samothrace, the Victory statue of classical Greece that had been found broken and forgotten, but now had been pieced together and reinstated. Emilia sees in Nike an image of victory despite destruction; Nike, maimed and mutilated, is no longer a victim, but alive and victorious. Emilia Fogelklou writes a jubilant hymn to her, which makes everyone who has read it always associate Nike with her. Klara Johanson, the eminent Swedish critic, wrote several years later from Paris: 'Every time I visited the Louvre I worshipped by *your* Nike and felt close to you. She sends a spring storm through one's heart.'[8]

Emilia's many impressions in Paris were often contradictory and confusing. She did not find anything like von Hügel's refined Catholicism or his courteous kindness, in spite of the introductory letters he had given her. The French thought it most unnatural and a little suspect that a woman on her own was travelling in order to study. In England she had been treated as a lady; in Paris she simply introduced herself an *étudiante* (student), a class evidently on the lowest rung of the social ladder, and treated accordingly. But she found even this an interesting angle from which to observe the rest of humanity. She made her own contacts. But she needed a good deal of humorous willpower. 'How one person in me laughs at the other! That feeble creature who doesn't want to look up strangers, who wants to take a cab home in the evenings instead of making my own way, who gets seizures by the way the Parisian horses are treated by their cab drivers...'[9] This 'feeble creature' observed everything – including herself – with alert eyes and found remarkable contrasts, there were 'fat-bellied, fat-spirited' abbés and others calling themselves Christians who seemed devoid of religion, while some atheists and other non-believers lived a dedicated life.

The evident stagnation in the Catholic Church she saw as partly due to its inherited traditions. And yet, it was here in France that the great modernist movement had begun with a burning enthusiasm and commitment that had found expression in *Le Sillon*. Emilia thought that people in Britain had hardly begun what France was right in the middle of – that Britain had no idea of what *égalité* (equality) could imply, but did charity 'amongst the poor'.

What Emilia was waiting for with breathless excitement were Henri Bergson's lectures at *Collège de France*, beginning at the end of November. Other Swedes had attended an earlier lecture series of this eminently popular philosopher for whom the essence of existence was both duration and change in constant flux; she knew what to expect. Here at last was a philosopher who spoke words that Fogelklou could feel akin to – intuition as the highest form of consciousness! In the packed lecture hall she was absorbed by the atmosphere: his narrow bird's face, husky voice, expressive mouth and eyes that gleamed like saturated points of light. His lectures have been reported as 'models of clearness and grace of expression'.[10] The ideas Bergson presented were a kind of confirmation of her own findings.

The following year, 1912, Fogelklou gave a talk on Bergson to Lund's theological society. Apart from the thirty assembled theologians, all men of course, quite a number of the old-fashioned local people had turned up to hear one of 'the evil radicals', i.e. Emilia Fogelklou. But they listened without ado and on the train journey home she spent such a jolly time with them that one conservative lady laughing and joking called to the theologians: 'She beats you hollow, all of you!'[11]

In her talk Fogelklou gives a clear and independent overview of Bergson's ideas plus a critique of them. She is herself aware of a certain one-sidedness in his teaching, but is also inspired by it. Fogelklou brings out psychological and religious analogies to his attitude: 'It seems to me that the description of the gathering of the spirit by which one turns inward and places oneself in the living stream of the present, has a certain similarity to the state of mind we call *prayer*.'[12] In conclusion she turns the spotlight onto all humanity in an urgent appeal: 'Eternity is not distant, it is in our midst. It acts with us. The person who does not add to it, dissipates it.'[13]

Home to Kristianstad to celebrate Christmas, she had a pause in the stimulating but tiring travelling. Relieved to be home, Emilia's 'shy hands' got busy with the bustle of preparations, baking and cooking as well as writing and editing.

But she felt tired and poorly during the winter. All attempts to find work seemed in vain. She had to find a post for the autumn before setting out on her travels again. In the end she decided to take whatever came along next, submitting to providential purposes. It turned out to be N.Beskow, head of Djursholm secondary school, who offered her a position and Emilia tried to see the positive aspects: country air, a mixed school and Beskow. But it was not what she had hoped for. She had dreamt of starting a Sunday school for poor working class kids in a slum area, making a contribution to her time. Instead she was to teach upper class children in an affluent garden suburb. It was all too cosy and her spirit rebelled: 'I know the meaning of "temptations" and could almost imagine the devil on the wall and that I would want to throw an ink-pot at his neck.'[14]

Italy

> *'Who has said that success is a necessary ingredient for us who struggle individually?'* Barhuvad p 170

So Emilia set out again on her way to the Italy that she had studied her Italian for so assiduously. She took the opportunity to stop off to see Hans Larsson in Lund. They discussed philosophy and science, Emilia absorbing his words that William James and other philosophers had softened the rigidity of scientific thinking.

On her travels Emilia did not miss any opportunity. So she stopped off in Munich to visit art galleries and in Dachau to see a painter she knew. Then the tour took her through Riva, Verona, Venice, Florence, Siena, Rome, Naples, Bologna.

The beauty of Venice was overwhelming. If Paris had opened new registers in her emotional as well as her intellectual life, the architecture in Venice added the dimension of beauty – with attendant exaction: 'When one is bursting with happiness and joyful eye-feasting, it is very strange to travel absolutely solo,' she comments.[15] They were just celebrating the 50th anniversary of the unification of Italy. Where she was sitting high up in her room above the piazza, surrounded by a multitude of mirrors she could observe her loneliness multiplied, unable to feel part of the general euphoria far below:

> It's so wonderful here. Just that I should have been here with you. With whom? With you, whom I've never seen. You who found me, you who never doubted, who never forgot, you who should have enticed the sun in my nature, who should have eased my melancholy and helped me emanate your spirit in thought and action ... But you have made me the most ordinary person of all; in looks, gestures and understanding. Unless you will it, no spark of life gleams in me. I can never decide things for myself, be intelligent on my own. I am just your rag, always aware that I am nothing, nothing, but a void in the

world that it pleases you to fill or empty according to your wish. ... I don't know anyone as lonely as you, the headmaster said once [in Gothenburg]. How much more lonely am I not now, after all the things I have had to leave on the way?[16]

We may surmise that the 'you' Fogelklou is addressing has a religious implication, refers to God or Jesus. But it is also likely that it is coloured by a missed person, someone she has loved. Four years earlier Emilia Fogelklou had fended off her memories, thinking about the one who looked back and was changed to a pillar of salt. Then she had urged: 'Ahead! ... memories will turn you to stone!'[17]

Now she must after all confront her past: that she in some way lost her youth in wanting to follow the calling she felt consigned to her through her 'Revelation of Reality'. It had taken her on a path of self-denial and solitary searching, without her still having found the task she was chosen for. That day she wrote a poem reflecting her feelings:

> A child I was. I did not know myself.
> You met me, came and found my soul.
> A lonely child that came too late to the feast of life.[18]

All her meetings with people, all her study and preparation for her vocation, seemed to have come to nothing. She was left with a teaching post at Djursholm which would earn her crust, but which she hardly regarded as a proper task. She was also alone. Her brothers and sisters were now all married – Emilia was the only one without a family of her own.

> So was my way since then not like the one of other women. No love-play, no home, no children, nor love for me alone.[19]

After this moment of insight, Emilia did not relapse into self-absorption for the rest of the six weeks in Italy. She filled a hundred busy pages in her diary with all the interesting places, meetings and lectures she went to, wrote innumerable letters and a number of newspaper articles. She spontaneously loved study and contact with people. Maybe the deep lack she felt in her personal life spurred her to live all the more intensely in the moment.

In Venice she had relished the architecture and bridges, the play of light and shadows. In Florence she discovered Fra Angelico's free-spirited and joyful paintings in the many little cells in the San Marco monastery. The pure lines of his designs made an indelible impression. Her enthusiasm is overflowing in a letter to a friend:

> Isn't Venice, Verona, London, yes, even Paris just 'bosh' against Firenze ... Just to tell you that the morning in the San Marco monastery was worth all difficult waiters and all starchy shopkeepers and all peculiar beds and mealy dishes and all money and more than that ... Oh, Ninni, Ninni, you see I do understand Fra Giovanni so terribly well.[20]

And many years later it was Fra Angelico's frescoes that she chose to illustrate her children's book *Befriaren* where the full-page illustrations take up as much space as the text.

The Italian postal service lost her letters of introduction to important contacts which therefore never were made. But on a poster in Firenze she read about an international conference on philosophy which was to be held in Bologna. By this time Emilia must have been rather tired of anything to do with philosophy and lectures, but struck by her 'scholarship conscience' she decided to go there. It was evident that she began to feel home-sick. A professor from Uppsala was on the list of participants but did not turn up. 'Had he come I would have rushed to give him a hug', she confesses.[21]

She did feel at home at the pleasant boarding house in Siena after all the philosophising. This was the town of St Catherine, the medieval saint that Emilia Fogelklou had really looked forward to getting to know a little closer. She appreciated the physical presence of St Catherine, the wax cast of her head, dead at the age of 33 (about the same age as Emilia was then), and the place by Fontebranda, the clear well of water where she had experienced her vision. With characteristic humour Emilia notes that she herself had no divine inspiration here, just that she could see all the rubbish at the bottom of the well, and she helped a laden woman carry her burden up the hill.

As often before Emilia had reason to reflect over the fact that all 'visions' are involuntary and can never be commanded. 'But when I look out through Porta Fontebranda across the tremendous landscape in the spring sunset, then my soul drinks in the earth, the air, the sun, the sea, the living blossoming trees like in my childhood. Could Catherine's vision have been more beautiful? It inaugurated her life task. Is there one for me?'[22]

Emilia Fogelklou carried this rhetorical question always with her. Expecting life to provide an answer one day.

⸻

In Rome Emilia made several visits to Casa Santa Brigida, where the Swedish Saint Birgitta had died in 1373, for long talks with Sister Elisabeth Hesselblad who headed a new branch of the original Birgittine Order. Emilia Fogelklou found these conversations very stimulating, when Sister Elisabeth recounted her way to the Catholic faith and to St Birgitta. They also provided excellent groundwork for Fogelklou's later Birgitta studies and clarified her thinking for a book like *Protestant och katolik*.

Assisi was the next stop on her journey. Emilia arrived in pouring rain, missing the person who was to meet her, and had to take a cab to one of the overcrowded hotels. Here she was met with the greatest incivility, assigned a bed at an exorbitant price in a windowless cubby hole for all the electric bell system of an expensive hotel. There she lay with no light, having to listen to the ringing of hotel bells all night. No wonder she felt extremely irritated and angry! But for the next few days Emilia was overwhelmed by her dreadful sense of shame not to have risen above this physical inconvenience just in Assisi, the native town of her beloved saint – where she was to have practised St Francis' *perfetta letizia* – the perfect joy.

Medan gräset gror I & II

It was during this Olaus Petri journey that Emilia Fogelklou heard from the publishers that they had accepted her manuscript for

Medan gräset gror I & II.

The two parts of this book are made up of essays on different themes that had occupied Fogelklou for a number of years. It is important in her production, as it is the first gathered expression of her attitude to life, reflected in the most varied subjects from the beginning of time to her present day. The wide selection of topics is representative of Fogelklou's copious areas of interest – from Classical myth to modern poems and contributions to contemporary discussion on teaching methods. The earliest essay, dated 1901, is on Walt Whitman, whose *Leaves of Grass* must have influenced Emilia Fogelklou's own choice of title with its subtitle of *En bok om det växande* (A Book about Growing). Whitman was at this time hardly known in Sweden, though he had for many decades alternately fascinated and offended the Anglo-Saxon world with his free spirit and innovative poetry. The third edition of his *Leaves of Grass* had challenged puritan morality by the addition of the cycle of poems 'The Children of Adam' with its erotic element. In her essay Fogelklou makes an elegant defence where she cites the Bible for the body as the Temple of the Holy Spirit (1Cor.6.19). Why should sexuality then not have its share in this earthly sanctuary? Emilia Fogelklou never abandoned this, for her time, very liberal view that the love-act could – and should – be sacramental.

All the extensive quotes of Whitman's poetry are Fogelklou's own renderings. She is the first Swedish author to have presented him in her country, where the first selection of his poetry in translation was not published until 1935.

Fogelklou admires his method: 'His ear is so incredibly sensitive to every pulse of real life. He does not give up until he has been able to elicit something out of every phenomenon.'[23] In Whitman Emilia Fogelklou finds a person who incarnates the qualities she herself aspires to. And indeed one can see in her description of the poet an (unwitting) image of herself, something that Hans Larsson has pointed out in his study of Fogelklou.[24] One senses how Emilia has put her head to the metaphoric earth to listen for all the hidden creativity taking place therein, so that her writing really has become 'a book about growing'.

Emilia herself believed that *Medan gräset gror I & II* expressed her view of life in a higher degree than any of her later works, especially the section entitled 'Attempts at understanding', short religious-ethical essays which actually represent the thesis she had presented at Nathan Söderblom's seminar in 1909. Emilia Fogelklou retained a life-long preference for these essays, and although she was to publish another 30 or so books and pamphlets during her long life, she regarded them all as 'just dilutions' of these early essays.

If 'Attempts at understanding' numbers no more than 80-odd pages, the material is all the denser. In it Fogelklou had exposed her 'Revelation of Reality' to the scrutiny of university studies – and it withstands the test. It had even grown stronger by her acquisition of theoretical argument: she is now able to counter logical reasoning with her own certainty of the enduring quality of spiritual values.

The titles of these short essays are evidence of the message they carry: 'With all one's mind and all one's strength', 'Life against non-Life', 'Every one and everything – the here and the now'. It is a question of giving all of oneself in every moment:

> It is now more important than ever before not to live in a dream, but live a life, not to copy a type, but create new human life out of Divine reality, not to divide oneself into two worlds, but live *all one's life* in the body one has, *religiously*, actively, personally, *within* time and space, not beyond them.[25]

This could sound a little too austere, if it wasn't a question of an act of love: 'We should constantly try to widen our world by loving more, and therefore also within us encompass or carry more of the whole richness of the outer world.' Fogelklou is well aware that this is not an absolute demand, but relative to individual potential: 'Surely we humans carry an immensity of unconscious, as if unborn powers...'[26] Emilia Fogelklou strove for the rest of her life to waken people's awareness of them.

The book didn't sell very well. Perhaps some found the searching light too sharp. Others found the style heavy. Fogelklou's thoroughness sometimes overshadows her clarity of phrase and her line of thought is hard to follow. Reviews were positive but vague. The theologians had nothing to say; they kept silent.

However, the book did not elude the finely tuned sensibility of the essayist and critic Klara Johanson (popularly known as KJ), who sensed quality regardless of person. In 1913 she writes to a friend: 'How scandalous it is that Emilia Fogelklou, this neglected genius, hasn't come to my notice before now! One with whom I can speak "with soul laid bare" to use her own words.'[27] And when contact was established, Emilia self-deprecatingly writes to her new friend: 'You see I am like the amateur poets, only appreciated by their acquaintances.'[28]

In Djursholm

In spite of Emilia's vision of Lucifer on the wall, the time in Djursholm were rich years in many ways. The school built on a liberal tradition, now under the headship of Natanael Beskow, who had previously given up his Art School studies for the cloth, but had found it too restricting and had gone his own way as a preacher outside the established church. His free attitude to tradition made him and Emilia natural soul-mates. It was his personal wish that she should join the school as a teacher.

Djursholm at this time was the gathering place for a number of gifted people. This was of course long before the TV age, and even radio broadcasting was not yet established. People created their own entertainment. Evenings with 'The Gang', the reading and entertainment club, where they composed songs and playlets and where musicians were always available, must have appealed to the side of Emilia which was 'clown and joker'.

A bill had just been passed providing state pensions for all, a cornerstone for all subsequent social reform, but the workers' situation was still desperate. In Djursholm, once called 'The Christian Cream Cake' by a bishop, Emilia obviously did not have any opportunity to realise her dream of creating a Sunday school in a slum area for grubby little street urchins.

But children are children even if they happen to come from well-to-do families, and Emilia worked on making her teaching lively and involving. But it was the Religious Education that caused her most anguish, as it had in Gothenburg. She never could feel that she did justice to the subject. She got excellent results and was highly commended for her work, but in some way she felt as if 'life had forgotten' her[29] *Medan gräset gror* had not led to any debate and made hardly any impact. She was a neither a successful writer, nor was she a prophet. What was her 'task' really about?

When her inner world felt dry and infertile, she went out into the open where the breezes could blow new zest. It sometimes happened that she felt strangely helped by intuitive experiences, like the time when she felt as if she was walking hand in hand with other women in a long line, warmed by the contact with her 'human sisters'.

And the women did need their mutual sisterly support. In Finland women had been given the vote as early as in 1906, Norway followed in 1913 and Denmark two years later. But in Sweden women did not get the vote until 1921 and Fogelklou was 42 before she could go to the ballot box. The concept of women's inferiority was so well established that most people did not react very strongly to the fact that women had no vote. But for thinking people the situation was like a practical demonstration of Weininger's quip that 'woman actually does not exist'. The question of pay was further evidence of woman's neglected position in society. Here Fogelklou had an unsought-for opportunity to demonstrate her position. Her outstanding contribution as a teacher had been observed by the school board who wanted to raise her salary to 3000 crowns per year (= c.£300), i.e. an increase of 50% on her annual 2000 cr. But the rise was intended as an exception to the rule and not as a general principle for women teachers with her qualifications. Fogelklou found this unacceptable. She could not bargain with her belief in equal rights for women – and refused the offer. So she kept her ridiculously low pay, while a less qualified male teacher received almost double the salary. Emilia Fogelklou's comment was that at least she had given the gentlemen an opportunity to reflect on the matter, which they had not done before. 'They think that I have done this not for my own sake but for "women". I think that I have done it as much for the men.'[30]

Iceland

Despite her meagre salary Emilia had managed to pay off the rest of her student debt and her friend at school had faithfully copied out all the morning prayers which formed the material for *Allvarsstunder II*, published 1913. Emilia drew a sigh of relief and exclaims in a gleefully exuberant letter that now she can afford to go to Iceland to 'mug up on Icelandic' as a continuation of her postgraduate studies to which she now added Old Norse. She was also researching material for her teaching of History of Religion in Sweden. The boat to Iceland set out from Copenhagen. There chance arranged one of the many meaningful meetings Emilia experienced in her life – on board were two eminent Old Norse scholars who put Caedmon, Cynewulf and other poems in her hands. She was amazed to find how close the Anglo-Saxon culture and language was to the Old Norse one. Here she had the first versified interpretations of the Old & New Testament in Anglo-Saxon, a unique document of the transition from paganism to the Christian faith, in that the poems are not only a rendering of the Latin into the local language, but a transformation of the whole concept and imagery to the vernacular. The form is the traditional epic with short lines and extensive alliteration.

The first fruit of Fogelklou's study was the essay 'Old Poems', where she also gives the first translation of chosen texts in Swedish. Here Christ on the cross is not the suffering one who has taken the sins of the world on himself, but the conqueror, as he has gone to his death of his own free will. This Christ à la Viking is given names like 'Ring-giver', indicating the generous lord he is, and he is served by his twelve 'earls', who are described as 'heroes, rich in honour, brave in battle' etc. One does wonder if the disciples would have recognised themselves. The cross itself becomes an image of victory, 'the splendid emblem... Creation shimmers in its glow.' Fogelklou appreciates the bold relish of these descriptions, also the graphic Hell where Satan rules, whose words fly like venomous sparks, with a glint of humour in his complaint of only getting rejected souls sent down to him. And Eve in the poems is strong and independent. She alone takes the blame for disobedience to Our Lord.

Apart from the evident literary and cultural merits of these old texts, they also offered Emilia a link in the chain of the development that she so eagerly sought. It is by poems of this kind that the Scandinavians were first introduced to Christianity in a way that they could understand. The exchange of symbols from Thor's hammer to the cross of Christ could take place fairly painlessly. But the great stumbling block and lunacy lay in that one now had to forgive, instead of avenging an injustice. Fogelklou was to see this conflict between the pagan and the Christian ideal, Thor's combat with Christ, as particularly relevant to her time – the essay was published just as the first World War broke out.

IV A Wrecked World (1914–1921)

> *'when the world is bleeding and every spark of life must go to reconciliation'* Barhuvad p 192

In the summer of 1914 Emilia Fogelklou was out walking in the hills together with a woman friend from her Uppsala days. They slept in barns enjoying the fine weather until the day when all the bells of the district began tolling. With the outbreak of war all of Europe was caught napping. Most states had not realised the gravity of the political tensions and those who did were quite naïve in the question of the realities of war. People believed in a *blitzkrieg*, a 'lightning war', which soon would decide the outcome. Nobody was prepared for the drawn-out trench warfare and the many slaughtered millions. Emilia pored over the newspapers, but information was brief and scanty. Sweden was neutral and the general population relatively indifferent to what happened over in Europe, but something in Emilia was beginning to smoulder. She saw events in the outer world as an expression of people's inner apathy. In September she writes:

> You see, I'm sure that with this ruined world God must send a wave of life that forces people to know the *reality* of God in quite a new way. So that they can't stand prattling pleasantries about God, that they have got from books. God's own fire must be cast out into the world, regardless of the wretchedness of us as tools. We *all* use – I too of course – the

words 'God' and 'prayer' etc. as if they were harmless relics, instead of hazardous realities full of vital energy.[1]

Emilia struggled on during the autumn with her teaching in the Djursholm idyll which felt more and more alien, at the same time as she continued her studies for a Ph.D. degree in the history of religion in Stockholm. Christmas 1914 was gloomy at home in Kristianstad where Emilia was alone with her elderly parents. There was an acute shortage of food which, together with her father's advancing cancer, blighted the feast – as the canker of war blighted the world. As an unexpected gleam of light there came a parcel wrapped in blue paper from an unknown sender. 'Please understand that I am sending you this manuscript as a sign of what we have in common. Not the poem in itself, the lines that run this way or that way – but the very reality behind them.'[2] This was the first Dante *canto* in Arnold Norlind's interpretation that he had thought of sending to Emilia. He had never met her, but thought of her as a distant 'Planet sister'. It would be a long time before these two celestial bodies converged and yet many long years before the spark of love would ignite that space. But the Dante *cantos* that came dropping through the post on and off for years to come would continue to open freer and more hopeful horizons in Emilia's life, then curtailed by darkness within and without.

The Hague 1915

'But still the hopeful star shone over the foolishly wise enterprise'
Barhuvad p 197

One felt powerless before the catastrophic escalation of the war. Could not the women of the world unite for a concerted effort? But they did not even have a right to vote in the world ruled by men. Before the outbreak of war some active women had planned an international congress of suffrage, which was to take place in the Hague in the spring of 1915. Now the bold decision was taken not to cancel it but take the opportunity to gather the world's women for a congress for peace instead. Fogelklou was one of the thirteen Swedish delegates.

The Swedish delegation at the Hague Conference. Emilia Fogelklou is in the centre (5th from left at the back), her friend Elin Wägner is on the far right.

Her father had just died in February and despite the company of other delegates Emilia seemed a solitary figure, dressed in mourning, jolting on the hard wooden seats of the third class carriage down through a Germany already ravaged by war. She listened to hollow-eyed fellow passengers describing the war in a monotonous monologue of misery. The reality of war was here so much more pressing than all the news reports Emilia had read. All the same, the women gathered for their peace conference with great idealism and loyalty for a cause that cut across national barriers. They had an example to follow. The congress took place sixty years after Fredrika Bremer had addressed her appeal to all women in *The Times* of 28 August 1854 against the Crimean war. The small article had then been met with total lack of understanding. Women had as few civil rights at this time as then and Aletta Jacobs, who had taken the initiative over the Hague Congress, pointed out that women could work effectively for peace only if they had political equality. If they were now so united, what would they not be able to achieve once they had the vote? Boldly they presented their message in personal visits to the heads of state in several countries. The women saw the war as having been started rather by mistake, it was a barrel of gunpowder that had accidentally exploded – amongst nations, armed to the teeth and fuelled by mutual suspicion. Nobody felt responsible, but neither could any of the war-lords be persuaded to make peace.

The women's peace effort ended pathetically. It was ignored, a devastating blow to their high hopes. But there were some positive outcomes. The Women's International League for Peace and Freedom was formed and is still active today. The Hague conference became an initiation for some who devoted the rest of their life to peace work. The Swedish journalist and author Elin Wägner formed a lasting friendship with Marion Fox in Quaker organised relief work in the badly damaged Ruhr district after the war. The close friendship between Elin Wägner and Emilia Fogelklou was to develop much later. The war had directed a searchlight at the spiritual state of humanity. Emilia realised that every person had a share in the responsibility for what was taking place. She had to scrutinise her own inner life and found it lacking. Old boundaries had shifted in the shattered world. She had no burning torch to light the darkness of this new world, barbed with uncertainty, only a small flickering flame in a threatening void. Before she could act she must have inner clarity. The darkness of the world was also the night of the soul.

FRED OCH FRIHET

Pax et Libertas
GRUNDAT 1915

MEDLEMSBLAD FÖR INTERNATIONELLA
KVINNOFÖRBUNDET FÖR FRED OCH FRIHET – SVENSKA
SEKTIONEN   NR 1 MARS 1965 ÅRGÅNG 39

Swedish branch of The Women's International League for Peace and Freedom

Sweden during the 1914–18 war

The World War not only caused an old order of society to crumble – hopes and ideals were also rolled in the gutter. The dream of international solidarity between workers went up in gun smoke. Many pondered on human nature and its metaphysical dimension.

Also the Social Democrats were in danger of a rift. The party had been firmly anti-militarist ever since the 1890s. When they now realised that a general strike against the war could not be effective, they had to choose tactics: to continue their pacifist policy or accept the general national idea of a strong defence. From Europe came disquieting reports of toppled thrones and governing 'workers' councils'. The differences became more entrenched within the Swedish party, but there was still a strong anti-war faction, supported by several intellectuals. Emilia Fogelklou waited in the wings, alert and watchful, prepared at any time for peaceful action; her pronounced pacifist position was quite rare at the beginning of the century and for a long time thereafter.

In 1911 a 'landslide' had occurred in Swedish politics when the ruling party decided to put off the building of a warship that the government had voted for. In the strong conflicts between left and right, the king took the part of the farmers who together with other right-wingers supported Germany and a strong defence. There was violent rhetoric between the parties, the Conservatives were particularly vociferous, denouncing peace efforts as 'meddlesome' and internationalism as 'lily-livered'. This intense political debate could not leave any thinking person unmoved. For many people it led to a profound examination of themselves and their position. People had been rudely awakened from the romantic nationalism of the previous century – the time now demanded a more energetic social commitment. Many also felt the need to get a perspective on the stormy present by finding their way back into the past, to a time of lasting values.

Hans Larsson's several outstanding polemical articles ran parallel with his stories from his home village. In both public and private policy one of his deepest concerns was to do justice to his opponent in the belief that even opposite points of view, if one plumbed the deepest current, would converge. Emilia, who had already at their first meeting 'got on splendidly' with Hans Larsson, found this to be in total sympathy with her own faith in people rather than in their views, as in Larsson's suggestion that 'one cannot gain a full understanding of ideas and questions until one has understood the different sides of the fighting.'[3] At its deepest level Larsson's fiction is both philosophical and religious in that it attempts a reconciliation with evil, working towards a unified view of existence.

In order to get a perspective on the situation and clarity as to what role she could play, Emilia also looked back into history. But for her it was not to scenes from childhood, but to other times of great turbulence. One such time of destruction and ruin was when Israel was in Babylonian hands. Twelve years earlier the prophets of the Old Testament had become wonderfully relevant to her after her own spiritual break-through. Now their significance had become universal to the world. But how to put this over? Fogelklou needed time for reflection until a course of action 'requested' her. She therefore took a year's leave to continue her study of the history of religion.

It was a question of awakening people to a new *perception*. But how? Emilia did not really believe very much in preaching 'on the outside', but more in the transformation that came from within. But she also recognised that people needed to be roused to debate and insight. For her own part Emilia felt it was more important to write than to speak, except in her teaching, of course. She had never been tempted to want to join the clergy. But as the first woman to have a degree in theology in Sweden she was often asked her opinion in the matter of women priests. The question didn't really interest her. Not that she had anything against the idea and naturally thought a woman should have as much right as a man to the profession. But in her view the most important thing for a minister was his life's work, not the robes of his profession. Many women carried out such pastoral care and teaching without any official title. But until the Church recognised this, what did it matter if many higher professions were closed to women?

What the time needed in her view was a vision to follow, not an argument about rights. And she points out that the great creators who have released a new wave of spiritual life have not been ordained but 'ordinary' people: a Jewish cow-herd (Amos), an Italian merchant (St Francis), a Nordic chieftain's wife (Birgitta), a German monk (Luther). Their inner calling had nothing to do with a profession, it was an inner compulsion that had been created by their view of wholeness where everybody has responsibility for each other, regardless of race or sex; where ultimately things are a unity. Emilia Fogelklou did actually harbour a deep distrust of the public office: 'Often professional religiosity reveals more of the ghost of piety, its discarded dress, rather than of life itself.'[4]

The year in Kristianstad

'Now I'm beavering away as fast I can, sometimes in "the mire of despondency" and sometimes enjoying the work.'
letter 4.12.1915

When Emilia Fogelklou took leave from Djursholm for 1915–16 she had a feeling she would not return. With her in mind the head had suggested to the governors an alteration to the statutes, so that an academically qualified woman should be allowed the same salary as a male teacher. The proposal was voted down. Emilia felt humiliated – not only by the governors' decision, but by the fact that she could not rise above it: 'My pride is writhing at this decision which cuts off all hope of any career for women.'[5] Fogelklou had never from the first felt this post as a real task. Her sense of alienation increased – in spite of golden moments with pupils and colleagues she now longed with all her being to be free. 'When I compare how I felt at my Gothenburg school ... with how little room Djursholm has in my world, then I think it is h.o.r.r.i.b.l.e. Would be tempted to say that I have never actually been in Djursholm!'[6]

Thinking of her mother's great loneliness Emilia did not want to continue her research in Stockholm, but chose instead to tackle her long-planned text books which she could write in her home town. Her father, generous and carefree, had left no provision for her mother whose circumstances were now much reduced. She was dependent on the financial assistance of her children.

During the year with her mother Emilia had undisturbed time to work, but in other ways life was hard. Kristianstad was not very inspiring with all its soldiers and rather petty small-town atmosphere. Sometimes she suffered from its 'Kristianstuffiness'. She missed her father, all the walks and jokes, discussions and even his short temper that used to cause an occasional brief rumbling storm. Emilia was 38. Death and old age inscribed their images in such clear and intrusive detail this second winter of the war. In spite of all her good intention and the joy that was also part of her nature, she could see no light or way forward. She asked herself if she was suffering from *acedia*, 'the dark night of the soul', that the mystics spoke of. In *Arnold* Emilia tells of a dream from this time which felt worse than any of Dante's scenes of Hell, but which she then did not connect with her own situation:

> She was walking in a country, where there was nothing but big piles of fine grey dust to be seen. Someone said to her: 'These are the seamstresses that have stitched themselves down.' They had never done anything except sew and sew, and this is what happened to them. A couple of drunks came past. A dead thumb, pierced by a needle, tumbled from one of the dust-heaps. And with a coarse joke one of the men kicked the dead remains of the all too busy seamstress.[7]

When you consider that Emilia's most thankless lesson at school was sewing, and that she had supposed her wearisome study of theology was her 'embroidery', the task she felt she ought to take on because it was the most difficult, it is not hard to see the dream as an image of her life. The dead thumb pierced by a needle, disdainfully kicked by the drunkard, is likely to represent her unrealised sexuality, a woman's life wasted away in constant work for others. During this time Emilia woke every morning with long bouts of weeping, which could only be stilled by her mother's gentle solicitude. Emilia could not understand her state, felt silly and small with her mother whom she had gone to look after. Now the roles were reversed, but then her mother was given a role she so well understood: the care of a child who needed her. During the day Emilia was her usual self, however.

Emilia's personal distress was like a reflection of the world situation. During the war the churches were filled as people sought some kind of answer to a situation that nobody understood or could see clearly. Even if the realities of war did not penetrate to the large mass of the population, the shortage of food and soaring prices were keenly felt. Rationing was introduced far too late, not until 1917, and as a consequence the black market flourished and many went hungry while others hoarded. During 1915 Fogelklou was offered the opportunity to take part in yet another peace initiative, which Rosika Schwimmer had managed to persuade the car king Henry Ford to finance. An international peace committee was to be based in Stockholm and Fogelklou selected as one of the four eminent Swedish delegates. Remuneration was magnificent, 2800 crowns a month, a sum many would find magnetic. Emilia was put off. To receive more money for one month than her annual salary (2000 cr.) for a peace action in wartime was warped, she felt, and she declined the offer. With typical humour she wistfully writes to a friend: 'Soon I'll have to count my fortune in the money I *could* have made.'[8]

Fogelklou's intuition about the initiative turned out to have been correct. The disunity between the participants from America was already rife at their arrival in Stockholm and no unified work was achieved. The whole expensive undertaking came to nothing.

As she had declined the peace committee Fogelklou set out on a lecturing tour to the rural population to tell them about the history of the peace idea and other international co-operative projects, talks packed with facts and inspiring examples that people should know about and which might appeal to their imagination, good will and work. This was her own initiative. Mystic she was, yes. But one that believed in practical action. She addresses herself as much as others when saying: 'Just to enthuse is not nearly enough.'[9] Her sense of mission, however unfulfilled, still informed her days with purpose, imparting an impressive dignity by its dimension. The same year she had written to KJ:

> I have had the sense of a great task – it does not
> leave me. Though you and I and everybody else can

see that I so far have done nothing. But it ties me to the immense inner chambers of life, makes the measures boundless and prevents me from being overcome by human frailty or human greatness.[10]

The Hague Congress had intensified Fogelklou's sense of personal urgency. The war was the outer reality that drove her to an intense working effort 1915–16. Her inner charge was always with her; in the fusion of these two her creativity almost became explosive. Between intervals of stagnation, her work progressed like a storm wind. To her diary she complains of her 'wretched working method' where she alternately despairs from lack of inspiration, then races ahead when it finally comes. Whatever her method, it achieved results. In the autumn of 1915 came the book *Förkunnare*, about the Old Testament prophets, followed by three more works published in the following year.

Förkunnare

'our language has so far lacked a work that so confidently has brought out the fundamental thoughts of the OT heroes and at the same time created such a living context for these remarkable and strange characters who stand like rocks in a turbulent sea.'
Sydsvenska Dagbladet 21.2.1916

Förkunnare was really something new. Right across the centuries the prophets now came to life with a new and intense relevance. They too had lived in a disintegrating world. In the collapsing Israel they had made themselves the voice for the responsibility that the people themselves must shoulder for the catastrophe that had overtaken them. Their message was valid now and had to be put over so directly and simply that people could accept it. The prophets were examples of people who actively and passionately responded to the troubles of their times. Fogelklou did not aim for esoteric learning or Christian dogma, she wanted to reach out to all people and her preface ends: 'This book quite simply wishes to draw attention to some historical characters that our time needs to meet.' Thus Amos, Isaiah, Jeremiah, Ezekiel, Job and others pass before the reader, more alive and accessible than they had ever before been presented in Swedish literature.

Fogelklou's pen is not burdened by her thorough knowledge; she has no ambition to transmit all she knows. It is the individual struggle for divine awareness in a time of inner and outer disintegration that she wants to depict, rather than to document the historical course of events. She felt personally close to a character like Jeremiah, understood his obedience to a higher task, however uncertain its outcome. Reviews were all positive: praising her grasp of the subject and her easy style, one of them recognised 'the power and the fire of the old prophets',[11] but a present day reader might find the style a trifle poetically exaggerated in places. The Church periodicals did not comment; Fogelklou had been far too personal in her interpretation of the Bible. *Förkunnare* was the only book by Fogelklou to be reprinted within the year. The second edition was published in 1920.

Förkunnare was soon followed by the next publication *Från hövdingen till den törnekrönte*. This book consists of two long essays, the first of which, 'Old Poems', had been written before the war. Now the image of how early Christianity developed is followed through history with the essay 'From Chieftain to the Crown of Thorns'. The Norsemen had understood Christ to be simple, sound and victorious. In subsequent ages people began to long for his human warmth at the same time as they became more aware of his suffering. Thereby followed a sense of sin and guilt, of human responsibility, a change of heart that is personified in the charity and humility of Bernard of Clairvaux. It is with a feeling for Christ's particular relevance to the time that Fogelklou ends her little 'war-book': 'While millions slay – and still pray; hate – yet sacrifice themselves, it seems as if Christ is calling louder than ever "in the desert of the world" to be heard through the discord...' These words Fogelklou used as a motto for the book, a sign of how urgently she wanted to arouse people's awareness and responsiveness. But more was needed to rouse the Swedish people from their lethargy. In her diary in May 1916 she mutters about 'the piously sleepy deference and the unholy sleepy indifference' that both needed to be transformed into some kind of action. Her way was through writing.

The next book was *Från längtansvägarna*. During her Kristianstad year Emilia Fogelklou also had time to collect and look over some of her essays from 1911–15. They describe people that she had met on her travels and their faiths. The five essays 'from the inside of Paris' are striking miniature portraits of some of these. As a unifying thread in Fogelklou's work during these years we find the spiritual seeking and sense of responsibility of the individual faced with world war. She clearly saw that the personality of any individual was formed in childhood and hence child education was a more central question than ever before. There was a crying need for practical suggestions for educational reform. Ideas were thronging through her mind at this time and she was unceasingly pursuing her research. She drew up plans for no less than five teaching books. The first in print was *Ur fromhetslivets svensk-historia*. With this book Fogelklou presents a continuous story of the religious history of the Swedish people. She had worked on it for four years since the beginning of her teaching career in Djursholm. The style is concrete, clear, matter of fact and yet engaging. It is not just a 'masterpiece of packaging' as one critic wrote, but also of fresh and innovative use of personally collected material. She herself had mixed feelings about the fruits of her labour. The book provides excellent source material for teaching, but never fulfilled its intended function as a text-book for schools. In her enthusiasm for the project, Fogelklou felt herself to have overshot the mark – a pioneering work, yes, but too thorough to be used directly in teaching, it seemed.

> While I'm working body and soul to build bridges,
> to help bring out new thoughts just *here* and just *now*
> … well, then I'm still being regarded as some blue-

eyed impractical dreamy romantic without any contact with reality.[12]

In *Legender från Sveriges medeltid* Fogelklou collaborated with two other prominent specialists of the period. The collection is effectively a rediscovery of a religious tradition that had been abruptly interrupted by the Reformation and that we had only recently begun to recover. Here we meet with miracles, omens and premonitions as part of the everyday world of ideas. Fogelklou translated half of the 60 legends into modern Swedish. This work gave her a unique insight into the spiritual aspect of medieval life in Sweden – these legends were part of the favourite, most loved and most read literature for several hundred years. Here was to be found inspiration to imitate holy men and women, here was the battle between good and evil, God's mercy and Satan's power, in graphic detail. This work provided excellent groundwork for the book on Saint Birgitta and *Från själens vägar*, where the chapter on legends provides a fine analysis of all the varied expressions of faith, 'for legend requires that every experience of the spirit be expressed in concrete terms.'[13] The legend has long been a scorned genre due to its lack of historicity, but it was never intended as a historical account: 'It *depicts* rather than describes.'[14] In the modern rational world it is rendered redundant: 'The new sense of reality has torn the old dream web to tattered shreds.'[15] And Fogelklou puts in a pertinent plea in her question: 'Where are the legends of our present time?'

Birkagården

'We longed for the people on the other side of a great gulf...
We guessed that this gulf was imaginary.'
Ebba Pauli *Birkagården* 1918 p 18

It was in the spring of 1916 that Emilia was invited to travel up to Stockholm to lead the first course for seasonal workers, the so-called 'painters' school', for a few weeks. She knew the lively atmosphere there from before, having taken part in its activities from the beginning. Birkagården was the first attempt to create a 'settlement' along the lines of Toynbee Hall in London which Emilia had visited on her scholarship trip. She had then observed the appalling plight of people in cluttered slum areas. To relieve the worst privation a small group of Oxford students had created the 'settlement' of Toynbee Hall under the guidance of Canon Barnett. Settlement is the name given a place where educated people settle in an industrial area to share the conditions of the workers and try to improve their lives through practical work, studies and local politics. In Sweden at this time there was affliction but no assistance for the industrial workers. But there were people with initiative. One of them was Ebba Pauli who had also seen and been impressed by the work at Toynbee Hall. She and Natanael Beskow, both experienced professionals, took the initiative over the Swedish settlement, strongly influenced by Nathan Söderblom's practical Christianity. Beskow, whose sermons in the Djursholm chapel had drawn a large congregation out to the garden city on Sundays, found, like Fogelklou, that the atmosphere amongst the wealthy villas was rather rarefied. He was longing for a more down-to-earth task in the smoky air of rubbish tip and factories. It was on the outskirts of Stockholm, in the slums of Birkastaden, that they rented a small flat, in the autumn of 1912, close to the industrial area and the city's waste disposal facilities. It was a dream taking shape. Emilia Fogelklou, who had helped in her spare time from the very beginning, has captured the atmosphere:

> Everything that is born out of longing and renewed listening, begins like nebulae or seeds, like stars or trees. And it is only when this has become dense or grown into a trunk with a crown of leaves that one can begin to study its structure.[16]

Vision became history, and 'where history is made, it always starts with people'.[17] Dagny Thorvall (Tove), Emilia's friend from Uppsala, was a valued worker from the start. When she visited the local cafes and drinking houses to spread information about the new centre of activities, she was told by the regulars that if it was about Jesus or abstinence they weren't interested. The Church and the new rationing of liquor were not popular amongst the workers. But they came! First the children in hordes to the 'book room', soon followed by their parents. Longing for some occupation other than physical labour they came, tired after a long day's work, but willing to sit down in the school room and study – Tove who taught languages marvelled at their 'savouring the subtleties of French like confectionery'.[18] The purpose of Birkagården was never 'to dispense charity'. It was more about the contact created between people across an abyss of social divisions. To Fogelklou's – and Birkagården's – good fortune a small donation secured a salary sufficient for her to able to start full time work in the autumn of 1916. Thus began one of the happiest periods of her life.

> You know, on October 1st I'm moving into a little cubby-hole opposite Birkagården with my own old furniture from home. Have such a strong sense that I'm beginning a new phase of my life.[19]

Happy to leave her post at the grammar school, Emilia at last had found the work with people that she had been longing for ever since finishing her studies. Here she was amongst workers in shoddy clothing and sodden shoes. For them she had to find a new way of teaching the history of religion, English and psychology. The usual phrases, especially for religion, lacked all meaning for them. The need to find a new language was pretty universal; in her diary she notes: 'Now it seems to me as if the Lord wants us stripped to the bone, all of us theologians, socialists, idealists or agnostics, who have had whole wardrobes of words to wear and use.'[20]

Like Tove she found that the labourers possessed an impressive thirst for knowledge: one wood-yard worker recited rules of grammar while carrying planks. Emilia experienced more immediate and practical contact with workers than ever before. Overcrowding, poverty and drudgery were concepts filled with a new and concrete meaning. Just as the Hague Congress the year before had widened her views on the question of peace, she now had a new insight into the world of workers. She was surprised by the undisguised animosity against the upper class that she sometimes encountered. She could well understand it, but felt it was frequently founded on ignorance. Now she devoted all her 'might and main' (her own expression) to create contacts that would bridge the social divide, giving impulses to new attitudes and ways of thinking. The atmosphere could get very tense in discussions on controversial topics, but there was also good fellowship.

The needs in wartime were the same for all. The shortage of food was severe. The staff at Birkagården had carrot soup and carrot pudding or whatever could be fished out of the big barrel of pickled mackerel in the cellar, sharing their provisions with their clients. Tove commented, amazed: 'If the fellowship between sinners *can* be such, what about the fellowship of saints?'[21] People dropped in – the door was open to all.

The war years had their moments of drama. Ivan Oljelund, editor of the anti-military left-wing paper *Brand* came one day to Emilia Fogelklou's 'painters' school' just when she was reading Socrates' speech in his defence. That same evening Oljelund was arrested for his attempts to organise a general strike against the government's preparations for war. Emilia Fogelklou for her part saw little use in official work for peace. She realised that psychologically the peace-effort had so much less to offer than war, which appealed to the heroic side of human nature: 'they all go out to war *thinking* to *die for something*, rather than to kill.'[22]

Instead Emilia devoted herself to the here and now of Birkagården. As always it was people who interested her, not theories. She entered a phase of intense creativity, scarcely finding time to sleep. Lectures, evening classes, people's lives. Here at last she was able to realise her long-dreamed-of Sunday school; then family evenings started, study circles, more people. Emilia was interested in everything and everybody, the many lives that touched her during this time figure briefly in *Barhuvad*. Now she had no time to write her diary, but used every moment, often even the tram-journey, while some friend paid for her ticket, in preparation for the day's lectures or study circle. But however she laboured, she found more joy than toil in this rich and rewarding work. Soon the workers formed their own association, ABF (the Swedish equivalent to the British WEA) with which Birkagården began a collaboration. One year Fogelklou shared her work between these two institutions, where she also knew how to captivate an audience – demonstrated by the fact that during the autumn of 1917 she gave a series of 13 lectures with an average attendance of 250! The workers were so keen that they started their own study circles in the subject she had introduced, the Psychology of Religion.

At the same time she somehow also managed to continue her own research. 'Behind me I have the healthiest, happiest year of work that I've ever had', Emilia discloses to her diary.[23] In spite of her stunning output of four books during her previous year in Kristianstad, she still felt thwarted; now the work at Birkagården released new spiritual energies. For Emilia ultimately believed more in practical effort than in intellectual achievement: 'The great and difficult problem for me is that it's not *the word* alone that must be counted as creative, not literary or rhetorical expression, even if this is absolutely charged with life and creativity.'[24] But her days at Birkagården were already numbered.

Interruption

In July 1917 Johannes Liedholm died. He was the husband of Fej, Emilia's older sister. Fej, unwell herself and without any income, was now a widow with a little son Rickard, 'Titten', who was Emilia Fogelklou's godson. Emilia kept hoping that Fej's finances would work out without her assistance. She could just about manage to pay towards her mother's keep on her meagre salary. But times were hard. Of her siblings her oldest brother was the only one in a sufficiently secure position to be able to help. But he had a family and Emilia had a quite extraordinary ability to take on other people's burden without asking for help from anyone. She also had a good education which she felt as an obligation – so in the end it fell to her to provide for Fej and her son. At first she felt like a porter who had suddenly been landed with a heavy piano on his back. It almost broke her. She realised that she must leave her beloved work for a better paid post. In her diary she gives vent to her anguish: 'Reading Job, lying in the ash mire like him, asking "Why?"'[25]

She could still remain for a couple of terms at Birkagården where the food shortage became more acutely felt, due to failed harvests and minute rations of milk, bread and butter. The Swedish people starved. Then the Russian revolution was followed by Finland's declaration of independence in December 1917. Celebration to have cast off the yoke of an alien power! But the triumph was a poisoned cup – the country was torn asunder by a civil war between the Whites and the Reds, and sympathies for the different sides also split Sweden. People canvassed for volunteers, gathered arms, medicines and food. Pacifist attitudes yielded to the crisis, even Ellen Key pleaded for armed forces for the Whites, in a petition signed by Selma Lagerlöf herself – Emilia Fogelklou declined.

Time weighed heavily at Birkagården. Tove could hardly keep going, especially since the government had refused a licence for a voluntary ambulance with which she could have helped. Emilia was silenced. Her answer to external conflicts was, as always, to turn inwards, seek the deeper reasons for people's foolish actions. She never signed a petition, never joined a political party. But when in a paper a member of the Swedish Academy lampooned a group of women who had appealed to the government to try to find a peaceful solution to the conflict, Emilia was provoked to reply. With simple dignity she points out that his cock-sure confidence of being in the right was just the sort of attitude that gives rise to misunderstandings and war.

Seen from the outside Fogelklou was coping competently. Her private world was a different story: 'The hidden howl within is probably connected with the pain of having to leave this place – a world where I meant something to people and where all my powers were used.'[26] But she supposed that there was something new she had to learn, and so she accepted the post as College Teacher in Kalmar. She wanted to live in obedience to a higher will, and like the most patient pack-ass she took on the burden of others as well as her own.

Kalmar Castle

'How can one reach from word-gods to God's words?' By 'word-gods' Emilia Fogelklou is implying the set and deadening expressions people use in talking about religious matters. The question of integrity in the use of words reared up again at her very first visit to sound out the college one lovely day in May 1918, when the bay was a shimmering blue and Kalmar Castle reared its silhouette with turrets and spires as if to bid her welcome. Emilia attended some lessons and immediately realised how limited these young country-girls, the trainee teachers, were, in stark contrast to the critically aware and more mature clientele at Birkagården. With the workers she had been able to speak her mind freely, but here in the conservative rural area she found the atmosphere so very different. Here she felt that she must remain silent, listen until she discovered a language that they could understand. With a suppressed sigh and half a smile she admits: 'It always seems to me as if I could love better on the left than on the right – a grave limitation!'[27] In the summer of 1918, while the war was staggering to its end, Fogelklou gathered her strength for a supreme effort – the book on Birgitta, the Swedish medieval saint: 'Just because of the woe of the world it's as though I am gasping to transmit a flame of life into the mass of the people.'[28]

St Birgitta, medieval woodcut

She was given leave until October to work on her book on Birgitta. All summer and long into the autumn she devoted all her time to it, totally entering into Birgitta's world. Perhaps Fogelklou had never before identified so with any historical person. She found Birgitta wonderfully alive in her vivid battles with the devil. Time had rationalised the belief in him away, but Fogelklou regretted the loss of the devil as a graphic image for the evil we have to contend with, inside as well as outside ourselves. In war-time especially he was evidently at large in the world. Birgitta fights over someone's soul with the devil or an evil spirit, never giving up until he lies defeated in the dust. As far as her efforts are concerned, he is not allowed a single cosy corner where he can doze undisturbed.

Fogelklou spent September 1918 in uninterrupted work at the university library in Lund, staying in Hilma Borelius' empty flat while Hilma took care of the fruit harvest in the country. This was the beginning of a deep and life-long friendship. Hilma Borelius was the daughter of the philosopher Johan Jakob Borelius – and a formidable intellect. As the only woman doctor in the history of literature at Lund university she was habitually on her guard against her male colleagues and 'the wives'. But in Emilia's company she found an equal, and in breaks between harvesting the fruit she came to visit Emilia for long nocturnal conversations on all kinds of topics, from politics to aesthetics. Emilia, who was busy writing, found Hilma's company impressive, opening vistas as from a high mountain peak. Many years later she sat by Hilma's deathbed in January 1932. 'You must let them know where I belonged,' Hilma whispered to her friend. Which Emilia did, writing an obituary in *Tidevarvet* in 1932, and she was entrusted with the task – honourable and laborious – of editing and publishing Hilma's posthumous book *Klarnad syn*,[29] for which she wrote the introductory chapter about her friend and what she stood for. After Hilma's death Fogelklou wrote a tribute to this rare personality – unaware that she also describes many qualities that could be applied to herself:

> Hilma Borelius' life is not only important as an individual destiny, though it is unique and captivating as such. It was a whole era of women's struggle that was embodied in this finely tuned, complicated, fiery and clear sighted being[30]

Kalmar

'But I wanted at least to die fighting, die alive'
letter 18.4.1919

With the end of September the enjoyable days of study were over. Emilia Fogelklou must away to Kalmar to shoulder the yoke of teaching yet again, under rain-laden clouds in the gloomy time of the Spanish flu. This severe epidemic had been raging in Europe and was now decimating the undernourished Swedish population. All October the rain poured down while the bells never ceased tolling for the dead. The college had to close for a couple of weeks because of the flu, giving Fogelklou a little respite to continue her work. To help her with her household chores Emilia had a country girl of giant strength and happy temperament who in ignorance used the whey cheese as soap and in carelessness cracked the china. She never had the patience to queue for hours for food, neither she nor Emilia could cook whatever little there was, and Emilia thought it likely that lack of butter and undernourishment were contributory factors to her later eye trouble.

The autumn was heavy. The war was still rumbling on, but she could not bear to engage in any public pronouncements: 'instead of talking about how desperate one feels and how dreadful everything is, I choose to stand by the fireside concocting a kind of potion that could be health-giving.'[31] Emilia is referring to the Birgitta book, where she gives of her very best, as a counterbalance to the state of the world. But she was hard put to get it finished with her heavy teaching load of over twenty lectures a week plus four morning prayers. As they were held as early as seven o'clock she had to get up before six to gather herself for the day's work. She also found that her predecessor had not adhered to the prescribed historical teaching of the Bible. It thus came as a shock for the students to see the Bible in the light of new research, especially a group of girls who had got caught up in a fundamentalist revival movement and recently had been 'saved'. They sat with their hands covering their faces during Emilia Fogelklou's lessons, silently praying that they might not come to harm by her teaching.

For a person with Fogelklou's resources it must have seemed strangely meaningless to waste her energies on such teaching. She oscillated between disgust, despair and – sympathy for the 'little girls', which is what she called the young trainee teachers. She comments laconically that 'the situation sometimes became a little trying'.[32] No wonder she felt torn: 'I don't *want* to work with a squint, in case the slightest chance should signal the possibility of returning to Birkagården.'[33] She felt strangely imprisoned also by the expectation that she as an RE teacher should set a good example and attend the Sunday service in church to hear their 'excellent preacher'. She absconded. In this tight corner Emilia Fogelklou's colleagues were a great support, mostly the excellent Head, Augusta Westerberg, who guided her through all narrow straits with great skill and tact and took the impact when she was able. She was wise, a traditional Christian, but unprejudiced and gave Fogelklou her full support. Not only over the unattended church services and her radical teaching – Emilia Fogelklou's interest in the labouring population and *Folkets hus* ('the People's Palace', where workers could congregate) was also disapproved of.

The eagerly awaited peace came at last in November 1918, but there was great anxiety for its consequences. Nobody cheered. Emilia never managed to put down roots in Kalmar. She never moved her own furniture there. Every spare moment she struggled to finish her book on Birgitta, which at last could be sent to her publishers in February 1919. Bemused, she writes: 'I have been so pressed with work that I'm toiling like a fagged out horse without looking one way or the other, or enjoying company or thinking of clothes.'[34]

With *Birgitta* safely out of the way Emilia could devote her energies to ideas about Religious Education, which was in desperate need of reform. The prescribed curriculum still required the students to learn large tracts of the Bible and Catechism by rote and Emilia Fogelklou detested the resulting rattle of texts. To tackle the conservative attitude in Kalmar was to her like digging through rock: 'It's like blasting your way through a tunnel – the trouble is that I have so little dynamite.'[35]

Fogelklou sought to make her existence in Kalmar meaningful by feverish activity. She took endless trouble to make her teaching inspiring, in spite of it being so repetitive that she wished she had a recording device to replace her voice. She developed a keen sympathy for preachers who were 'worn out with words' and felt something similar was happening to her. She thought of St Francis' words 'Too much preaching makes the spirit's feet dusty' and to save herself she shook the dust off hers by taking off to the nearby island of Öland at weekends, where she could recover in the silence of nature under the open sky: 'Lying in the heather by the sea hour after hour. Healing now, spirit free from dust. The elements give me a new sense of belonging.'[36]

How she needed those breaks in order to resume the weekly tussle with the timetable, early morning prayers and the country girls who thought they defended the Biblical image of Christ and his immaculate conception! None of the issues of the day had even touched them and the whole inquiry into the historical accuracy of the Bible seemed most unnecessary to them. Emilia was hoping that her time in Kalmar would be brief, that she would somehow be released from her financial duties to her mother and sister, but now even her younger sister Gert was in difficulties. Emilia began wondering if she was 'life-sentenced to be a meal-ticket.'[37] In February 1919 she felt such repulsion towards her repetitive 'gramophone-Christianity' that she felt physically sick. This spurred her to intense questioning of how the teaching could be reformed. 'After horrible affliction and unspeakable disgust' with the existing curriculum she managed to draft out some new ideas, but she didn't know when she would have time to develop them. According to these the children should first be told stories from their own time analogous with Jesus' method of teaching by parable. Only after such preparation would the children hear Bible stories that they then would be more likely to understand. Fogelklou would need considerable assistance for this work, for she wanted to find new sources, stories that might never have been written down, about ordinary people's striving for God and the heroism of everyday life. Now they should be collected and retold in a clear and down-to-earth style. Fogelklou made up plans for a whole series of teaching books and wrote to the minister of education, but she never received an answer. Women could be ignored, especially if they were introducing new ideas. But she did get an opportunity to air her schemes for reform in a lecture she gave at *Folkets hus* in 1919: 'It seems in some strange way as if my subconscious was involved in some unceasing and unappeased thought process.'[38]

The teaching did have its positive sides. Some students had become so fascinated by Fogelklou's teaching that they asked for extra seminars – and there was *Folkets hus* where she taught in the evening to local labourers and the workers' union. Öland continued to be a place for refuge opening wider skies over her teaching in college. But often it was hard going: 'It has been like walking through some strange thorny thicket where I seem to get nowhere and be of no use...'[39] Emilia was amazed to see her solid male colleagues teaching RE as many hours as she without the slightest sign of the difficulties she experienced in transmitting a holy heritage. She felt it as a betrayal of the most precious values to have to repeat the live, creative words of the Bible until they turned to dust on her tongue. Was she supersensitive, she asked herself, to react so strongly against the living spirit being worn down by habit?

> The new-fangled teachers, poor things, chatter so casually and inconsequentially without a trace of connection with their subconscious. Has any single age actually had less *education of the subconscious* than ours? Our time which discovered the word has not faced how absolutely crazy it is that educated people have a totally unknown, unirradiated, unexamined subconscious, while some little islands of opinions, party allegiances, word-trash etc. float around on the surface like the beads of fat in a broth – and are popularly regarded as the quintessence of culture!!![40]

Fogelklou continued dutifully to teach as well as she could, but she was getting very tired. Yet she was not released from her grindstone. In the autumn she was to start another academic year. *Birgitta* came out for Christmas in a de luxe edition, beautifully illustrated, and the first encouraging comments from friends were filtering through.

Birgitta

> *'I lived so closely identified with Birgitta...'*
> letter 10.4.1919

Sweden's only saint had been the object of several earlier studies that had described her life and analysed the texts of her Revelations. In the rational atmosphere of the time, Schück had dismissed them as having been caused by 'indigestible food' and her visions as being created by a 'grieving widow's sick imagination'. But nobody had taken the trouble to study the texts with such detailed attention and sympathetic understanding as Emilia Fogelklou now had done – Birgitta comes fresh off the page, a creature of flesh and blood; we feel her pulse in Fogelklou's portrait. She emerges as a good and clear-minded person who never had any 'pious' contempt for learning; a spirit too critically aware ever to pass for a 'holy innocent'. Birgitta is the 'mother of all souls' – her willingness never fails, she never meets anyone's need, male or female, without spontaneously feeling responsible, wanting to offer all her resources.

Birgitta is part of Fogelklou's research into the position of women which runs like a thread through her life's work, though never from an extreme feminist point of view. In this case the his-

Birgitta in editions from 1919 to 1973

torical situation serves to shed light on Fogelklou's own time. Birgitta made detailed plans for the religious order that bears her name. In Birgitta's order of service Mary, the mother of God, takes precedence. Emilia Fogelklou comments: 'The feeling of inferiority that has plagued and stunted a large number of women loses its sting by their affinity with Mary', a feature of the Christian faith that got lost with the reformation. 'There is a strange void for a woman that incarnation of God never takes place other than in a typically male shape!'[41] With this reflection Fogelklou is touching on a delicate subject, still controversial in our present time, some 80 years on, but now there is at least some debate, for instance on the question of women priests. Emilia Fogelklou's point of view was then so new that it was completely overlooked by her contemporaries, except for the learned historian Lydia Wahlström whose woman's heart was gladdened. She observes that Fogleklou has discovered Birgitta as a pioneer, an example to follow.

The fact that Birgitta comes so alive to the reader is of course due to the degree of Fogelklou's empathy with her subject. The six hundred years separating them melt away in the similarities one perceives between them. They are both strong, richly gifted women with a knowledge of being 'chosen'. They both feel for humanity and take on others' woes. Fogelklou writes of Birgitta: 'There is something in her that is always grieving. But not even this is inactive, her pain is a spur to action. It is not there for itself only, but as the birthpangs for something to come.'[42] The mystical insight entails responsibility. 'Inspiration is not a privilege, it implies a duty.'[43] For both Birgitta and Emilia the essence of mysticism implied not a turning away from the world, but involvement with it, and thereby an attempt to impart eternity into the present moment. Birgitta's persuasion of being God's mouthpiece did not save her from long periods of personal anguish, doubts and boredom. She, like many other mystics, experienced *acedia*, the spiritual torpor when everything seems dead and indifferent – again a parallel to Fogelklou.

According to the Catholic writer Sven Stolpe, Emilia Fogelklou's description of these elements of Birgitta's life 'belongs to the most important and beautiful work she has written ... Actually her Birgitta-book is also a book about herself ... written by the only author of our modern literature who herself has experienced the most elevated and also the most anguished spiritual states – who is herself a mystic.'[44] Thus the portrait of Birgitta merges with the image of Emilia in a kind of double exposure, providing us with an example to emulate. Birgitta had sometimes been called a 'witch' by her contemporaries for her uncomfortable soothsaying. At one critical time there was a real danger that she would be burnt at the stake. Emilia for her part was something of a 'wise woman' who had stood all summer and autumn of 1918 by the stove to prepare her health-giving potion for a world where all values seemed wasted by war. But for many critics the portrait of Birgitta was too personal, too 'unscientific' and different from the one handed down by tradition. 'The potion' had a mixed reception.

Protestant och katolik

If this little book is hardly larger than a pamphlet, its contents are all the more important. It is an independent analysis of the two major branches of Western Christianity. In a bold image Emilia Fogelklou describes the relationship between Catholicism and Protestantism as an axis of which the vertical arm is the Protestant, direct from God to the spirit, and the horizontal one the Catholic, supported and carried by the Church. The Protestant feels the individual responsibility more keenly, whereas the Catholic has a deeper understanding that we in a sense *are each other*; Luther's struggle with his conscience against St Francis' infinite sense of unity with creation.

Fogelklou is aware that this diagram is a simplification and limited as such, but on the whole it held true at the time of her writing. Protestant emphasis on the individual can lead to arrogance, putting mankind into the centre of the universe – but Fogelklou also points out its great advantage: a Protestant has full freedom to listen, learn and discover spiritual values from any source, whereas the Catholics were at the time bound to their church for religious experience.

On the other hand Catholicism in its worship of Mary provides room for an appreciation of woman that Protestantism lacks, especially in its Lutheran form. Where are the Protestant saints corresponding to Clara, Birgitta, Theresa, she asks. The paucity of feminine contribution was poignantly brought home to Emilia during one of her lessons when a young pupil said wistfully: 'But is the Bible only always about big men? Isn't there anything about little girls?'

In Fogelklou's view neither Catholicism nor Protestantism is enough in itself. Both attitudes are needed. This open approach goes deeper than a mere acceptance of Catholicism, beyond what concepts like 'tolerance' and 'unitarism' suggest. It reveals an attitude to life which the philosopher Hans Larsson has formulated as a 'confluence in love, not unity [between two things] but oneness [a single entity]. It is simply a different perception of religion than the most commonly accepted. Its essential characteristic is piety such as is expressed in a thousand forms, in action and contemplation, in strong and weak souls.'[45] One could say that Larsson here expresses the essence of what Quakers seek. When he wrote this essay on Emilia Fogelklou in 1935, she had been a member of the Society for a couple of years. It was a step on a path she had walked all her life.

Protestant och katolik was reprinted in 1937, considerably enlarged. In 1919 it was an element of the current religious debate. Almost 40 years after its first publication it was recommended for inclusion in the 1958 discussion on Catholicism in Sweden.

The spiritual state of Sweden

Towards the end of the World War and in its shattering aftermath, several questions were left in the air. People also felt renewed need for a faith to rely on. But the Church was no longer a solid rock to lean on – foundations were giving way. In 1919 a conference was organised at Sigtuna, the religious-cultural meeting place, on the subject 'The Spiritual State of the Church'. This could be seen as a continuation of the earlier 'Church in Crisis' debate after the devastating blow the natural sciences had dealt the traditional

Christian faith. Now the situation was further aggravated by people's rootlessness and their sense of living in spiritual wilderness in the wake of the war. What did the Church have to offer? The contributions were printed in three parts.

'From Dogma to Gospel' was the title of a talk given by Emanuel Linderholm, a young minister, causing the strongest reaction with a chorus of disapproval from both the pious and impious who were shocked by his direct questions: 'Is there a higher reality? Is there a God, and if so, what evidence is there to make me sure of his existence, to help me see a purpose in this apparently meaningless life?'

Emilia Fogelklou was asked to contribute, but hesitated. Her experience of God did not easily lend itself to verbal expression. In the end she overcame her reluctance and resolutely spoke in support of Linderholm. His questioning was vital and had to be answered as honestly as he himself had spoken. Conventional language no longer convinced. Fogelklou's God was not one to be fettered in ready-made phrases; he is 'the Master who orders us to rid our spirits of all borrowed feathers ... and assume responsibility ourselves.'[46] Again and again she reminds us that life is our religion and the quality of it depends on what we are willing to stake.

During the autumn Emilia grew more and more tired. She struggled with teaching and extra commitments. She could not protect herself from people's pleas for assistance and had not the sense to spare herself: 'Now I've taken on a couple of months' extra lectures on the psychology of religion. No point in saying "I am a nut", I'll just have to plod on.'[47] But overwork was beginning to take its toll. Her eyes were giving trouble; they were sensitive to light and strangely dry, hampering her busy work. She had to start asking herself questions. Was it right to continue teaching at this post which she had taken only for the salary? She felt caught in a cleft stick: in doing what she thought to be her duty, she felt she was selling her soul.

Eventually it dawned on her that the question she was labouring with, about honesty to oneself and personal integrity, could be seen in a much wider context which was to do with a new type of culture and a re-examination of essential values. But she still had no alternative but to drag herself to college before seven every morning.

KJ (Klara Johanson) had already warned her friend Klou (Emilia) about her exaggerated sense of duty: 'You have the strange obsession in thinking you must justify your salary! I have never heard anything so crazy ... You can with a good conscience collect this paltry pay even if you play truant from all lessons. For your very existence and the fact that you deign to walk the Swedish earth and look at Swedish citizens with your radiant eyes is more than ample recompense.'[48]

But Emilia's 'radiant eyes', from which her spirit emanated so unforgettably for anyone who met her, were in a sorry state. These 'windows of the soul' were misted over. Doctors were puzzled. They could not agree on the cause of her eye condition, but at last conjunctivitis was diagnosed and Emilia went to Norway for treatment.

During this time of partial blindness she found inner clarification. She realised that there must be a way of earning the necessary income without having to continue a teaching that had become as abhorrent as her 'Revelation of reality' was sacred. But until a solution presented itself she must continue at the Kalmar college. Her eyesight did not improve – with this state followed a sense of unreality, everything seemed strangely meaningless and she hardly felt alive.

Darkness seemed to have invaded her life on all sides.

During the summer of 1920 she made her decision: because of her poor eye condition she would take a break from teaching. As a final effort she wanted to make one more attempt at a text book or reader for the teaching of RE on lines she could believe in, as a last contribution to her college teaching, hoping it could serve some purpose. She had had enough of listening to so many vapid lectures and sermons and continuing a teaching that she felt had 'fettered God's words'. She felt that such use of Holy Writ contaminated the message. With horror she recognized her own part in the process: 'I myself am one of the word-polluters. Woe is me!'[49] A new phase of her life opened with a cry from her innermost being:

> Plough deep, plough deep my heart's earth,
> Plough down everything that just turns to – *words*.[50]

Från själens vägar

'To lead a religious life is, from a spiritual point of view, not just to have seen the fire, but still be living close to it, just because it burns...' Från själens vägar p 174

Emilia Fogelklou herself thought she had a better grasp of the written word than the spoken. In spite of her eye trouble she managed to gather her many years of research on the psychology of religion into a collection of essays from 1917–1919, *Från själens vägar*. Two friends from her student days at Uppsala came to her rescue when her eyes gave out.

Already as a student Emilia had been fascinated by the philosophy and psychology of religious attitudes in William James' *The Varieties of Religious Experience* (1902). She had found James' pragmatic approach liberating, relieved to find a philosopher and scientist who allowed for the reality of the invisible or mystical world.

For this collection of reflections on spiritual life Fogelklou, like James, has gathered material from hidden corners of culture, old superstitions and dogmas. The apparently dusty or trivial is given fresh life in her interpretation and begins to gleam with the inspired glow of the first religious insight. According to Fogelklou there is religion in everything. Nothing is void of meaning or exists outside the boundaries of religion. For life *is* religion. Thus the religious perspective is not reserved for noble sentiments, high ideals or our best actions. It also includes human evil, our despair and our hatred, for in our negative impulses also there is an energy that can be transformed. It allows for the whole person, such as we are.

What then is religion in itself? There is no easy answer. Religion, it seems, lies in the intensity with which we live, how much we are prepared to offer. The religious attitude demands constant striving and seeking. Fogelklou quotes the T'ang Emperor's inscription on his bath-tub: 'Renew yourself daily' (1700 BC). Religious life needs constant attention, for 'spirits can falter, become ill and die, like bodies' – it is a question of 'gaining strength from one's God, otherwise there is death and stagnation.'[51] So everything depends on whether a person 'again can become nothing and let her/himself be created ... or if s/he at some point closes off the holy fire and wants to keep her/his lower self unconsumed and overgrown.'[52]

Fogelklou shares James' belief that the individual person's spiritual striving is of far greater importance for the spiritual life of the world than all organised religion. This puts an immense responsibility on each of us. We can no longer rely on 'good habits', for now one has to work on oneself unfailingly, turning all shortcomings towards the light.

She brings up topics from her earlier writings, but now with the experienced scholar's authority. After her lengthy wrestling with theological vs. scientific thinking in Uppsala, she can now calmly confirm that 'science' is as unscientific as the soul. 'Reality cannot be proved any more than spiritual life.'[53]

One dogma she discusses is the virgin birth which had been as violently attacked by natural scientists as it was fervently defended by theologians, and had caused her much anguish as a student. All theories seemed to obscure the interpretation that Fogelklou found most rewarding and now presents – the mystical: the virgin birth as a metaphor for the birth of the son of God in a person's soul. By this interpretation the speculations fall like outer shells round the core of symbolic meaning.

Hans Larsson has observed Fogelklou's rare understanding of

the inner life, how she as teacher and scholar above all is 'a listener to people', making observations with the 'freshness of the self-seen'[54], i.e. her work has the vigour of original thinking. She builds on her own experience in the description of two different spiritual types: the saint and the prophet. Undoubtedly she had certain qualities of both. Two years after the publication of this book Emilia was to link her life with a man whom many have thought to be a saint, whereas Emilia was seen as a prophet.

Från själens vägar was recognised by a few discerning critics as a central work. It was the first study of the psychology of religion in Sweden. But its major importance is still not widely recognised.

Sickbeds

> 'We were "dying every day" for weeks, months ... Every new attack has seemed like the end' letter 30.3.1921

The Board of Education commissioned Emilia Fogelklou to examine the teaching of RE according to the new regulations in different schools round the country. On her travels she acquired insight into other teachers' difficulties with the subject. Between her trips, Emilia made frequent visits to her home. Four years earlier it had been her mother's loneliness as a widow that had diverted her during a sabbatical year; now it was her mother's illness – the end seemed near. Emilia felt far from well herself, but despite everything, Christmas in the old home felt rejuvenating. In a jolly paraphrase of St Francis' exhortation to be joyful she writes to a friend: 'Mankind is meant to be *happy* – it is our "damned duty" and part of our Lord's purpose that we cannot escape from.'[55]

Soon there came news that her older sister Fej's illness had taken a sinister turn. It was for her sake that Emilia had taken on the post at Kalmar and now death seemed close, but had found a brave spirit to wrestle with and the end came many months later than the doctors predicted. Emilia's mother insisted on her going to her sick sister, so she left with a heavy heart. The following months became a constant round between Kristianstad, Malmö and Lund, home and hospitals, with bedside vigils. 'I have a strange existence awaiting Death. I am in such a strange conflict between "work" and "people", which for me must remain unresolved, as I don't wish to cut off either, above all not people! Like the "unmarried daughter" of past times I wander here like a great harmless poodle...'[56]

The mother was failing and died in April. Her sister still lived but was expected to die at any time. Emilia felt responsible for her godson Titten and planned a journey with him to Nanna, Fej's twin sister in Hexham, Northumberland, during the summer holiday. But against all expectation Fej lived through the summer and Emilia had to put off her plans in order to nurse her in Malmö.

It was a strange year when all plans for work, travel and eye treatment had constantly to be re-arranged. Fogelklou's leave of absence ran out in April though her 'conjunctivity', as she called her condition, still was not cured.

With her mother gone and her sister nearing her end and herself not in full fettle, Emilia needed her friends more than ever. With an uncertain future and the sense of her life leaking away without a real mission, she was under psychic pressure, not lessened by the fact that she was quite aware that her physical condition now as ever was a reflection of her psychic state. To KJ she writes some of her most spontaneous and open letters: 'When all is said and done I suppose it's the continued opaqueness of my own subconscious that I'm raging against. But one day the crystal will form – this is what I cling to even now, when I'm such unbearable company – even by letter, that an anchorite's cave really would be the best place for me. But am I not in prison since coming to Kalmar? What have I then to complain about? Verily, I am provided with all that is needed for the clarification process, it is just *the serenity of spirit* that is lacking.'[57]

The fact that this letter breathes energy and zest despite her state is possibly connected with another incipient friendship. During the spring Emilia had made a second visit to her 'Dantefriend' Arnold Norlind. Her eyes were slightly improved and she wanted a library ticket endorsed, eager to resume her studies at Lund university.

Six years had passed since the first brief encounter, when Emilia had looked up this unknown man who sent her signs from another world through the *Cantos* of Dante. But the first meeting had given no indication of any providential affinity. Emilia had then in the open door seen an unworldly creature with kind eyes, a little red-tipped nose and shabby checked trousers. They had seemed worlds apart. But the *cantos* had sporadically kept coming through the years and had now arrived at *Purgatorio*. Arnold and Emilia had occasionally exchanged letters. She knew he lived at a different address in Lund.

v Arnold and Emilia (1921–1929)

A late love

> *'All that was burdensome and hard dissolved in this peaceful and somehow joyful atmosphere. She felt her innermost self naturally revealed'* Arnold p 34

Now she stood there again at his door, on an impulse:

> Surprised and delighted he brought her into a room where all walls were covered with books. There were a couple of beautiful tall-backed oak chairs, a large desk and in the corner behind the door a simple narrow iron bedstead. Now it was so easy for them to meet. He talked and she talked. Different points of view and comparisons took them far and wide. It was as if they had flown to meet each other across the worlds. They understood each other's natures as never before.... Mi became strangely moved. The most embarrassing thing occurred: she burst into tears. And then she hurried away from him, vexed with herself to have spoilt something in itself so perfect.[1]

But she hadn't. The meeting had activated the latent friendship which now after a long winter sleep revives into the most ethereal bloom, though love has come late in their lives and the leaves soon will turn to autumn colours in the park where they walk. They are constantly meeting, they have so much to catch up with, she 42 and he five years younger. In Arnold Emilia discovers an incredibly joyful character 'walking the earth with such a light step' – but the slight huskiness that Emilia notices in Arnold's voice is the beginning of a tragedy which neither of them then could guess.

Both had each in their way hungered for the other half of their lives – without finding their match. Arnold had once been engaged to a young woman ... and Emilia also had an unfulfilled romance behind her from which she had taken years to recover. Now both stood with one phase of their life closing behind them and the future unwritten before them. Emilia felt as if they were two spirits in space without a foothold on earth and everything they talked about related to a past life.

Now Emilia gradually got to know this rare person's inner values. It was not Arnold's outward appearance that attracted her, nor his intellectual power. No, there was a *quality* that rose from unseen depths, an atmosphere of purity and goodness, an unconscious emanation of kindness and healing light. Arnold's company had now become an indispensable part of her life and gradually she pieced together his early history.

Arnold's story

Arnold was born as the fourth child into the family of a poor country vicar. He had an unusually solitary childhood, living in the bosom of nature, as if untouched by the hardships of life. The animals were his only company, he leapt with the lamb, calmed the untamed colt and befriended the dangerous dog. Arnold was a vegetarian from early on – he could not bear to eat his friends.

The poverty of the home was richly compensated for by the natural beauty of the vicarage setting. There was a large garden with a brook, bushes and trees where Arnold developed a fantastic skill in climbing. Light and lithe he shinned to the very

Emilia and Arnold walking in Lund. Illustration for Arnold 1944

top of the highest trees; on swaying branches he could swing right into the huge sky-ocean, preferably also at night high under the dizzying starry sky. When Emilia got to know him, she thought this experience might have provided the germ for Arnold's interest in world images and perspectives.

Arnold developed a passion for study – his interests spanning a great number of subjects – geography, astronomy, history, languages, aesthetics, literature and art. From this broad base germinated a doctorate (1912), a historical-geographical study of the Rhine delta up to 1500.

Light relief in Arnold's laborious study was the small gathering of friends that he and Ellen Michelsen started in 1911, called 'Infinity', with its symbol of a reclining figure of eight, as everything between heaven and earth was to be debated by the eight members, who for lack of chairs often reclined on someone's floor in front of the stove. In this circle Arnold was the great enthusiast, eagerly gesticulating his excitement at some literary discovery. A friend has remembered how: 'he loved such nature worshippers as Thoreau and Walt Whitman. It was Arnold who taught me to appreciate them ... Once when I visited him he offered me thin crispy pancakes that he had made himself. We had to eat them with our fingers, for it's only when you feel the hot pancake in your hand that they taste as they should, he explained.'[2] The fellowship between the members of 'Infinity' was close, they kept in touch long after life had scattered them to all corners of Sweden.

Arnold's approach to the opposite sex was the shyest imaginable – his first romantic attachment being to a singer for whom he harboured an undeclared passion for three years – with a longing so strong that he sometimes felt his throat choking with tears, which seems strangely poignant in the light of his later illness. Arnold himself realised that this inability to express himself was a limitation to his emotional life and for many years dreamt of being able to 'open the floodgates' to his feelings.

It was in the spring of 1911 that he met a young woman, Frida, and fell in love. Or rather she with him. And he allowed himself to be steered towards an engagement and impending marriage. It coincided with an extremely heavy academic workload that year which, together with the detailed demands of his fiancée regarding their future home, became too much. In spite of huge efforts to make it work, Arnold had to break with Frida the following year. For a long time he felt he was walking in the valley of death and understood that he should live alone henceforth.

The war came and Arnold was called up. He quite enjoyed his solitary and undisturbed watches on the coast, with Wicksteed's English translation of Dante in his pocket, and thus began his own rendering of *Divina Commedia*. It was at Christmas that year that he sent his first *canto* in translation to Emilia. During and after the war Arnold worked hard with his teaching and research. He was regarded as a skilful and popular lecturer; he debated current issues of the time and published articles on geographical and literary topics. But while his spirit feasted on the fruits of learning, his body grew leaner and lighter. In the food shortage of the war years his weight went down to 44 kg. But what did it matter? Was he not healthy? Arnold set willpower before everything: 'If a doleful destiny overtook you, would you not have the ability to transform it into something bringing blessing? Mark you, it depends on *yourself. Yourself!* Turn all you have of rage and passion *against* yourself...',[3] words that in their intense exertion of will both explain and cast an ominous light on how his health later developed.

Arnold Norlind's learning encompassed not only the classical languages but also their cultures – though his specialist field was historical geography he was also well acquainted with the political and economic conditions of the time. Now his aim was to give an overview and at the same time 'with a thousand little tongues' capture all the nuances within his area of study:

> I feel I want to be as universal as possible. I would like to love everything and be able to express this. I mean that there would be currents of love between me and things, also abstract things, so that their meaning would be clear to me.[4]

This mystical approach to scholarship is unusual at any time –

then especially it made Arnold an early exponent of what later would be called an interdisciplinary approach, a kind of synthetic thinking which chimed well with Emilia's since her 'Revelation of Reality'.

But after having been acting professor for four years Arnold did not apply for the post when it became vacant in 1916. What was the reason? At Emilia's question many years later he just smiled, never answered.

Now he was leaving university life; his future lay open and unknown before him. A nagging little throat complaint was the only hint of another destiny. But Emilia knew nothing about that.

Emilia on her travels

> *'I have lived in the company of death for so long. I feel I have so little life left'* Arnold p 44

In September 1921, when Fej's funeral was over, Emilia with her godson Titten undertook her long-projected journey to Britain in September 1921 and left the boy with her sister in Hexham. Emilia felt emotionally exhausted – her year-long close acquaintance with death and grief coupled with her eye condition had used up all her energies.

But she headed for London to look up old friends from her former visit and to study at the British Library. Worn out by all the interesting 'social' experiences that her recovering spirit had lured her to, she pauses by the large Ephesos frieze in the British Museum. In the perspective of this ancient monument with its representation of old myths, Emilia reviewed her life. Her quick jottings became a poem 'The Angels', with the character of a classical elegy in form and content. During the past year Old Reaper Death had been hard at work:

> Along the road lay hearts, homes and thoughts mown down.
> Her powers, clarity and light cut out. […]
> No living voice reached through the gloom.

But now Arnold's spirit had flown to meet her, a living being who understood her right into her very darkness. Emilia had never expected love to come her way. Now it was simply there – how sad they had not found each other before! She felt so old and worn, with nothing to give. But the angel of Love did not let itself be put off, but demanded its due. In silence then her spirit gave

> its impotence, its feebleness, its sorrow –
> that was all. And it lay as if dead, [...]
> but the air was brushed with the rush of its feathery wings.5

The running rhythm of the last line lifts the mood. All her life opened towards this unforeseen love. She must obey its command, however insufficient she felt. Earlier in life she had watched her own reactions too closely. Now she must forget herself in the presence of a high command. She wanted to be prepared, unconditionally.

During these autumn weeks their relationship ripened like the fruit in September orchards. Arnold wrote long loving letters to Emilia in Britain. Emilia was the Ariadne who was now to guide him out of his labyrinth of bachelor loneliness and break the shell of isolation round his personal life. The dream of a woman who could bring meaning to his existence had become a reality after many solitary years. And to his great relief he heard that his former fiancée had now married.

Emilia's spirits were also recovering: 'I have been so quiet and orderly and only kept 'good company', so I'm afraid my inborn wickedness is breaking out here and there. I hope it isn't catching!'6 Her 'wickedness' probably refers to the ironic humour with which she observes the curious way in which the British deal with their problems; the Irish question, the conflict with India, social ills – with a lot of talk and little action: 'a well-meaning grinding coffee-mill, largely ineffectual in respect of events, although it might serve the presumably good purpose of keeping them thinking they're achieving something.'7

A fresh vitality is breathing life into her languishing existence.

Meeting in Berlin

> *'Our situation is so strange, so singular. One could think we should have been brought together long ago'* Arnold p 195

Arnold held a scholarship that would run out in 1922, so he had to find work. Until something turned up he had a grant for a research trip to Italy to study old maps drawn by early seafarers. He planned to travel south in the late autumn. Emilia was on her way home from Britain via France. Surely their roads must cross somewhere? Travelling in post-war Europe was fairly easy and inexpensive. Three years after the war the worst suffering was alleviated and there was some recovery after the great inflationary crisis. The atmosphere was optimistic despite everything. Forty-two countries had joined the League of Nations and there would never be another war.

It happened to be in Berlin that they met, two sensible middle-aged academics – and had more fun together than they had ever had in their lives. They wandered from the Tiergarten's early winter hoar frost on endless walks:

> They now had to fill in all the gaps in each other's past history. They had met so few times in the outer world. Their lonely paths had run parallel in many ways. And when they now met both had completed a phase of their life … When their feet got tired with walking, they took to the nearest café … and when they wanted to refer to something previous in their conversation it was in terms of: 'What you said in the 4th café' or 'in the tea-shop with the fat lady' etc. Their childishness was unbelievable, genuine and bubbling. It was like making up for lost childhood play…. They were so amazed, so incredibly happy, these two old children who had stolen away from their ordered and self-denying lives to a little adventure that nobody in the world knew about except themselves.[8]

They nearly gave up all thought of other duties and continued together to Italy. With hindsight one would say: 'Why not! Perhaps their whole life together would have taken a different turn…' But no gentle goddess dissuaded them from their decision only to allow themselves just over two days together.

How should this small rock in the ocean of eternity suffice? The horizon stretched endless and unknown before them. Their life stood outside time and no earthly tasks tied them. They had to capture each fleeting moment – and they did! Nothing was lost or wasted on them in this brief time together. They both felt, intuitively, beyond the shadow of a doubt, that they belonged together. Emilia observed with a smile that Loneliness, which had been their companion for so many long years, was feeling quite a gooseberry!

But a sense of duty demanded that each should follow their prescribed path. So they said farewell, knowing they would soon spend the rest of their lives together and feeling as hopeful for the future of the world as for their own.

But almost imperceptibly fascism was growing under the leadership of a brilliant young Mussolini, and the following year it would gain in power with 'the march to Rome'. This city was now Arnold's destination. In the south his throat would be cured.

Arnold in Italy

But wintry weather and other snags steered things differently. In Rome there was no lodging to be found, and in spite of doctor's orders to rest, Arnold had to continue with three days uninterrupted travel in a draughty third class carriage before reaching Taormina. He took no notice: 'It was so easy. All the time I was carried by this incredible joy.'[9]

But his throat!

In Taormina his throat started bleeding, but healed after a week. Then he was heading for Florence via Syracuse in harsh wintry storms and wrote a letter in a feverish condition, the roads were well-nigh impassable: 'Poor horse was wading in water and mud, "Povero cavallo".'[10] In Florence the weather was wretched and the library where he was studying unheated, which put a further strain on his throat, but Arnold, with his iron will, allowed himself no rest. He did not believe in ill health. Back in Sweden his throat was 'bothering' – there was a wound that had to be cauterised. It was tuberculosis of the throat.

News of the serious state of Arnold's health reached Emilia in

Jakobsberg just outside Stockholm, where she was staying with friends. The same day she received a telegram that her brother Bie had suddenly disappeared in disquieting circumstances. She had reason to fear for his life as well as Arnold's. Beside herself with anxiety she restlessly paced the roads on an endless, aimless walk. Unexpectedly she was followed by an unknown large shaggy dog who not only looked up into her eyes, but eagerly and persistently began licking her hands. She never forgot the sense of a great mercy this strange dog transmitted to her – at that time she could not have tolerated any human contact.

It turned out that her brother had gone bankrupt and fled from his ruin and his wife. For months nobody knew his whereabouts. It is a touching tribute to the esteem he had for Emilia and the closeness of their relationship that when at last a letter came it was from America and addressed to her, describing his hardships and saying farewell – he intended to take his life. In the end this did not happen; Bie survived and his wife Agnes went out to him, living in the USA for a few years before they both returned to Sweden for good.

Both Arnold and Emilia had a basic great faith in providence and positive forces. Together they made up cautious plans for the future. Arnold was offered a teaching post at Birkagården on about a third of his previous salary, but they reckoned they could live on it. 'You can't believe how *life, life* and joy is breathing through me.'[10] Arnold fervently hoped for health, but out of consideration for Emilia he was prepared for a 'white' marriage i.e. with no sexual relationship. The doctor explained however that as his illness so far had been unusually 'dry' he was not considered infectious.

What was Emilia's attitude to sexual intimacy? A letter written to her friend KJ (Klara Johanson), who was not the marrying type, reveals her positive standpoint: 'I don't like you feel unqualified disgust at nature's arrangements ... As regards the vital energies I have nothing against the animal aspect, as long as it has its human context and doesn't act all on its own like the bodies of beheaded chicken. (Forgive me, dear chickens, that was a bit hard on you!)'[12]

To Emilia the boundaries between different kinds of love had begun to dissolve. She was finding that married love, maternal affection and love between siblings and friends etc. all spring from the same source. She was approaching the idea that 'love is just One Only ... Acts of nature in all creatures can only be symbols of this, and in how many lives aren't they stains on the symbol rather than evidence of its divine origin!'[13]

Emilia did not want to compartmentalise love in such a way that sensual love was accorded lesser value than the spiritual: the *eros* of eroticism was included on equal terms with the selfless caring of *agape* in 'the One' love. Emilia's concept of the sacramental character of the love-act differs significantly from Ellen Key's 'gospel of love', which replaces religion; a stance that Emilia found superficial and one-sided.

The next occasion when Arnold and Emilia could meet was at Whitsun at his sister Laura's home, quite close to the old vicarage where Arnold had grown up. There all clouds of anxiety were swept away by their turbulent joy of being together. He could show Emilia all his sacred spots from childhood. Most things were unchanged; the tall trees just a little taller, Arnold's 'houses in the wind'. He didn't take long to climb them and Emilia who also had been a tomboy climber was soon sitting on a branch beside him. Arnold's elderly aunt was there, worried to see such little evidence of courtship between them, but they mischievously foiled her expectations and their laughter rang amongst the trees in a mood of festive abandonment.

The Fogelstad women

'Inspired by joy and high spirits'
Siri Derkert in Kvinnor och skapande,
(1983, Women and Creativity) p 288

The spring of 1922 was the very time that Elisabeth Tamm sat in the library of her country estate of Fogelstad by the open fire with a small circle of friends – an outstanding gathering of professional women who were mulling over the effects of the recently acquired votes for women. After so many years of struggle and winning the vote long after their Scandinavian neighbours, the interest shown

Siri Derkert's homage to the Fogelstad group, sandblasted line drawing on the wall of Östermalmstorg underground station, Stockholm

by the majority of women was disappointing. They didn't know how to vote, and either abstained or voted the same as their husbands. Elisabeth Tamm, energetic and generous, sent a kindling spark to the group round the fire: 'If women are to make a mark in society they must be *capable* and *informed*. Do you want to take part in organising a training course for women this summer?'

So a new era was inaugurated, literally and metaphorically. The first residential course took place during four weeks that summer, soon followed by the start of a weekly paper *Tidevarvet* (The Era), a mouthpiece for issues raised on these courses which were open to any woman over the age of 20, free of charge. Emilia Fogelklou was on the advisory committee from the start, and the fact that she did not take part in this first course must have been due to her personal circumstances. In later years when life with Arnold did not absorb her time, Fogelstad became a second home for her.

Now she had other things to do.

The cottage in the wood

> *'What a little nutshell of a house they had and what oceans of books to pack in'* Arnold p 227

They had found Lillstugan (Little Cottage) to buy, surrounded by pine trees and with a south-facing veranda in Jakobsberg, just north of Stockholm. Good atmosphere for lungs and throat, they thought. After some building work the little house would be ready at the end of the summer when they would get married and move in. Arnold wrote the tenderest letters to Emilia, whom he described to a friend as 'a rippling spring' and explained to his surprised friend: 'We had such a rare insight into each other's beings, something of the nature of a vision. This gently grew...' And with the approaching wedding in mind: 'I have such a quiet, joyful contentment – as if the gates of Wonderland are opening.'[14]

But if the 'wonderland' held miracles, it was also of a very earthly nature, full of pitfalls. The builders had not finished on time, so their furniture had to be stored with friends nearby where they also lodged for the time being. In the end they decided to move into the half-finished cottage anyway, longing to have a home of their own, and with the wedding arranged for the last day of September. But then there was nobody to help with the removal, for everybody was out in the potato fields, busy with the harvest. So they got going on their own with the help of their friends. Arnold pulled books on a cart to the cottage and the stream of boxes seemed never ending. There were books on the veranda, on the stairs and in every room. Everyone was working and in their excitement nobody thought of how dangerous this labour might be for Arnold's precarious health. Nor did he have the sense to spare himself. With will-power you can achieve anything, was his motto.

Even an hour before taking the train to the little country church, Emilia still stood in her old cotton frock, unpacking cases of books. But she did have time to change before leaving. At the train they met Arnold's sister Laura and Emilia's sister Gert, who combined the roles of witnesses and guests. There were no others. In the gentle evening light of the church decorated with flowers they spoke their vows without the minister's assistance, as agreed. Then they saw the sisters off on the train and wandered the couple of miles home through a transparently serene September evening with the first stars glimmering.

In the cottage invisible friends and the housemaid had magicked the boxes away, prepared a table with fruit and deep red roses and lit a bright fire in the fireplace. Life was large and happiness

Lillstugan – the cottage in the woods

without end. Emilia would now have time to write. Arnold would work at Birkagården, sharing his enthusiasms in an environment that suited him. So they built castles in the air and planned for the autumn.

Their new-found happiness lasted precisely four days. Arnold suddenly lost his voice, could not produce a sound. How unfortunate to get a cold, just as term was starting, they thought.

It was no cold. The doctor didn't want to frighten them. To begin with he just said that Arnold's throat needed to rest.

Hard times

'But Arnold, aren't we what people call "happy"?'

Arnold's condition was worse than they could imagine. Emilia was eventually told that he had hardly more than a year to live with such a throat and part of one lung affected. This she had to keep to herself.

What was now going to happen to their lives, to Arnold's teaching and working with the people at Birkagården – and their economy? There was still no health insurance; all medical care must be paid out of their own pocket.

This autumn they were further tested with one misfortune following another. Arnold lost all his savings on a loan to a friend whose house burned down uninsured. He immediately wrote off to publishers who had previously offered him work, only to find that others had taken over. Arnold and Emilia, who both on more than one occasion had taken loans to help others, were sent an unbalanced letter from a well-to-do close relative who wanted to pre-empt any request for assistance. Arnold took this very hard. None but the very closest knew about their financial position.

They were alone with poverty and death in their nutshell of a house. Time had caught up with these timeless people and put an hourglass by their side. When would the sand run out?

For the time being Emilia could take on Arnold's teaching at Birkagården. But after that?

Both had admired St Francis' life of poverty. Now they were put to the test – could they live like the Brothers, who like the birds owned nothing in the world, but put everything into God's hands? They would try. So the two created their own secluded world, which Emilia describes as 'a sunny island, a coral reef in the ocean with its own laws, both those dictated by poverty and illness and those that were based on unfathomable riches.'[15] The thing was not to lose their foothold and avoid the sharp edges of the reef!

In Emilia's description of their life together in *Arnold* it is he who stands out as if transfigured. She found how he could lie in the early stillness of the morning, bringing a lightness to the coming day out of his own inner resources. Thus he prepared both his work and the atmosphere in which it was carried out. He was not allowed to use his voice, but banking on health, wrote articles and developed his teaching at Birkagården as a double act with Emilia, where he was the silent partner and she spoke.

But in the game of life with Death having such a strong hand, also Emilia's inner resources were brought out. 'I forgot illness, lack of voice, for in his company I breathed the purest air my spirit ever breathed.'[16] Far from experiencing the enforced silence as a hindrance to their lives, she describes it as a source of strength. It trained their sensitivity to atmospheres, 'vibrations', it became a means for new ways of interchange. They discovered an infinitely greater variety of means to communicate in silence than in the common way of using speech.

Emilia was not new to the appreciation of silence. Already during her European journey she had reflected on 'how silence was almost always best and how wonderful it would be if one could come as far as to give and speak wordlessly.'[17] To KJ she had written on the subject of company: 'Perhaps one should never *speak* but breathe a bridge so fine that one almost thinks it isn't there – but no, it's stronger than anything.'[18]

In letters to friends Emilia never complains about the burden of extra work Arnold's illness laid on her: 'No creature could have done my spirit more good than this marvellous soul, so filled with love and harmony, which I have been given the privilege to have by my side. I had never dreamt there'd be such a kind of spirit, so pure and harmoniously wrought that I am constantly surprised that such a thing is possible!'[19]

It was now not only a question of survival, which was tricky enough from several aspects, but to live meaningfully. There were two chairs in the 'book room' where they sat together under a roof light with a glimpse of the sky above, pondering their situation. They had no debts as such, but all savings had gone and they had very few means by which to earn money.

Together they drew up guidelines for their life: in spite of their precarious position they decided to take on only such jobs that were in line with their way of life, even if they were poorly paid, if at all, and never to work purely for money. When no solution seemed possible they would seek inner clarity together.

These were good principles to live by, but Emilia could not always manage to keep her anxiety at bay. At night her worries came out of their holes, assailing her. It was not just the illness; poverty pecked at her with impudent questions about things like food for the day and unpaid bills. Neither of them had been used to living from hand to mouth.

But Arnold had a gift for dissolving difficulties. When Emilia returned from her walk to collect the post, weighed down both by the burden of the post-bag and its contents of refused articles and bills, Arnold came to meet her with light step, would take her coat and shake it smiling. So he shook all the worries to the wind and continued confidently until Emilia's gloom and gripe at his childishness had turned to laughter and they could together face the trials of the day – in a lighter mood.

Playfulness was to them not just pastime but a necessity – without it they had not been able to live, only languish.

The child

> *'I'm also convinced that we too will be given the Giver's second gift, a child'* Arnold in a letter to Emilia 29.12.1921

They found they had everything that according to Luther's Catechism was essential for a contented life – except 'pious children, health and cattle.' They hoped for a child, in spite of everything! They weren't young, but it wasn't too late. Arnold, like Emilia, was very fond of children. For her the child had been central to her pedagogical study for many years. It was circumstance rather than natural inclination that had made her dismiss any thought of marriage and family.

Life took a different turn.

The first summer of their marriage they rented a cottage in the mountains where the high air and their hosts' abundant generosity were positive powers for healing body and soul. But from a neighbouring farm sometimes a woman turned up with a little sick waxen child. His parents were healthy, but they were nursing the husband's sister, ill with tuberculosis, who had kept too close company with the boy. During Arnold and Emilia's stay first the young woman, then the child were buried.

Lederåsen – the cottage in the hills

All this affected Arnold dreadfully. He saw his own fate

grotesquely mirrored in their neighbours'. He could not speak of it. Against the backdrop of the splendid mountain scenery Emilia read in Arnold's features a despair too deep for words. The dream of a child died with the insight that he must refrain from intimacy with Emilia. With his customary self-discipline Arnold still kept going with daily exercise and work on the Dante translation. But he did not speak of what was on his mind, and Emilia felt shut off from him and from the world, unable to approach him about what concerned them closest. And their money had run out; they did not even have enough for the return fare home.

It was the most difficult time of their marriage. In despair, Emilia spent one whole night walking in the forest. The white light of the northern summer seemed merciless, she saw no way to continue. But after some hours there came a great gentleness, a soft breeze with another message. She got up from the moss where she had been kneeling, feeling comforted. There would be a way out. And the morning post brought the repayment of a small loan plus an offer to Emilia of a lecture tour during the autumn.

The love between Arnold and Emilia was becoming more and more sublimated into a Dante–Beatrice relationship.

Continuing

> *'It was a question of balancing on the narrow bridge of possibilities between precarious worlds'.* Arnold p 234

So they strove on, Emilia on her lecture tour, Arnold at home writing to her every day.

> The priest and the dog
> earn their grub with their gob

she quotes in a gently self-mocking mood to KJ.[20] Arnold's letters to Emilia wrapped her in a magic cloak on her constant travelling. He had to accept the reversal of their intended roles – she the breadwinner, he waiting at home. Yet he continued his writing, textbooks for schools on historical and geographical discoveries and the translation of Dante. He could not bear any inquiries of his health and never touched on the tragedy of his illness, except in rare moments: 'With all my accumulated love, I had so terribly much longed to cherish someone. And when at last it was given to me, I was cast down and the one who needed looking after.'[21]

With the love that Emilia had released in Arnold he had many opportunities to lift her dark moments of impotence when facing their fate. Emilia could not bear to dwell on the thought of how Arnold's scholarship and learning was not put to use in the service of society, which he so longed for, and how this rich inner life was housed in so frail a body. She occupied herself to divert her mind.

By inclination and habit Arnold and Emilia were both diligent workers. Every morning they sat in silent and assiduous work between 9 and 12, each at one end of the large dining table, unless of course Emilia was out lecturing. The sun would shine in on their piles of papers and the light birch-wood furniture that Arnold had brought from Lund. The work was undisturbed by conversation and no typewriter clattered; both wrote by hand. At midday they cleared the table and then had lots to talk about over their meal. During the times when Arnold was not allowed even to whisper, they used little notepads and found playful ways to communicate with mime and gestures. Such humorous devices put a little gold rim on their days.

They complemented each other's interests and areas of research in a very useful way. Emilia especially found that Arnold had a gift for finding quotations and ideas for her lectures from his large library. Arnold in a long bright blue robe (a present from Emilia and a bit of a tailoring error, but adored by Arnold) sharpened her pencils and translated difficult Latin in a jiffy.

Arnold Norlind
Drawing by A Cassel

The new science

Due to circumstances in her childhood as well as a natural gift, Emilia Fogelklou had developed a clear and penetrating eye for people's inner worlds. As a teacher she had further practised her observation by seeking to see the children from their own standpoint. It was the psychological clarity in her talks on RE that made her ideas on teaching so innovative. Now psychology claimed its position as a new science.

Before the war Bergson's philosophy of intuition had been a dominant factor in Swedish cultural life. Now psychology became the fashionable new science. In the aftermath of the war it seemed to combine science with a philosophy of life. Freud's ideas had been introduced to Sweden in 1914 by the physician and 'souldoctor' Poul Bjerre who had travelled to Vienna to meet the great man. The method of studying the subconscious mind developed into a way of analysing life and culture as a whole, thereby having a huge influence on the post-war generation. A lantern was taken down into the dark underworld of secret sexual desires. By this light, idealism and elevated emotion were questioned; religion was seen only as illusion. The radical young student society *Clarté* initially adopted Freud's ideas uncritically, as did many others.

Fogelklou who always remained sceptical of mass movements, kept a certain distance. She retained her freedom in respect of all doctrines and also quickly understood the limitation of Freud's. But she also saw the relevance of the new ideas for the understanding of the human psyche. In a lightning flash she saw an interpretation that fitted her own early years: 'Poul Bjerre speaks of inferiority complex as a severely debilitating psychic factor. It burdened my whole childhood...'[22]

Liberating – and scorching. Fogelklou admits that the reading of psychiatric literature also had been difficult, tempting her to cry out 'That's not true!' when the most fundamental experience of her life was threatened by an interpretation of being a subjective fantasy, created by her subconscious as a surrogate for frustrated emotions. But even this she wanted to face, plumbing the very depths of her psyche, emotionally, intellectually, spiritually – until she came through in the end. For ultimately even this was religion, seeking a truth, however hard. She recognised its positive aspects: 'And yet I have been helped by this searing study. Not just because it could not turn my experience into an illusion, but because it became a sort of purgatory that forced me to make the effort of separating reality from the many clouded mirrors that have seen it.'[23]

Emilia Fogelklou tested the new ideas on characters that she had already studied in detail:

> St Paul and Birgitta and Luther, these self-examiners and explorers of the spirit, they certainly knew the cellar of the soul, just as the modern psychoanalysis does; they also knew how remorse and self-knowledge and confession can clean up down in the nether world, where the monsters of the deep were destroyed like the trolls† in the sun, and where the soul could be free and winged like a bird.[24]

In spite of certain limitations the new science was invaluable, for it teaches us 'how destruction can threaten an emotionally impoverished spirit and how conversely help and healing lie in the ability to love some ideal, person, animal or whatever, which can hinder egocentricity from laying waste a soul's potential.'[25]

Fogelklou therefore recommends a course in psychology for every RE teacher to enable them to study the great religious documents as an account of spiritual development and not only as historical texts.

In her earlier study of the Old Testament prophets Fogelklou had not wished to separate the spiritual from the temporal; in-depth psychology and psychoanalysis she saw as a valuable method for understanding a personality. To her mind, the subconscious and the spiritual were not opposites, but part and parcel of the whole character.

In Fogelklou's view the important factor was always the direct application of ideas to current situations. So she wrote an inter-

† Trolls are creatures of the night, known to burst if touched by the sun's rays.

pretation of the Sermon on the Mount with reference to the World War generation, ravaged by thoughts of revenge. The headings to her sections would stir any mind with their direct challenge: 'Is Jesus' way of life easier than the Ten Commandments?' 'Guard against gain!' 'People pass judgement like dogs or swine.' This and other equally arousing studies were published in an educational series. Only recently this work is gaining interest. Emilia Fogelklou and Hans Larsson have been named as 'two giants in the history of Swedish education' in a recent work on education.[26]

Fogelklou actually knew she was breaking new ground and saw her work as 'ahead of the concerns of both Christians and non-Christians just now.'[27] But she also had no illusions about whether her work would gain any general approbation. To KJ she writes: 'In this enormous Stockholm with all its authors... I, if someone even had heard of my name, am reckoned as some sort of bigoted manufacturer of the lowest grade of third class "religious" effusion, not even of sufficient standard for the cultural churchgoers.'[28]

Friendships

'Little Ola, we humans need to hold each other by the hand. Life is so windy, and our fingers get so cold and stiff if we don't warm them for each other.' letter 19.9.1915

Emilia Fogelklou's circle of friends was now as ever of enormous importance. She took a lively interest in others and had a real gift for friendship. Her bonds were warm and durable; Emilia really bothered about her friends and had a rare ability to share in their lives, always discreet about confidences. When they didn't meet there was lively correspondence. The friendship between intellectually and politically radical women was at the time almost a condition for survival. It carried them through crises and helped in making strategies for endurance in the patriarchal world with its lack of understanding, indifference or condescension. The women also relied on each others' support on the personal plane – rather heavily sometimes, as her letters to some friends reveal, when she ruefully refers to times in the past when she realises that her low spirits cast a cloud over her companion. Emilia ('Ili' to her friends) could not always control her moments of anguish and despair in the company of her closest friends. But she also had much warmth and tenderness to offer. Two posthumous collections of her letters have been published; she had over a thousand addressees. Evidence of Emilia's supportive reaching out is gathered in the substantial collection of her papers in Gothenburg University archives.

Her friends were surprised at Emilia's ability to empathise with each individual whom she questioned with real interest and whose circumstances she remembered in detail. To the very last she was a caryatid who supported and above all listened to others. What she wrote at the age of 73 was true for all her life: 'I think I'm turning into a large *ear*, that people speak or whisper into.'[29] She constantly carried the friends who needed her in her thoughts. With characteristic practical humility she said simply: 'It usually helps, you see.'[30]

But she could also put her foot down in matters where she disapproved. She made her mind up quickly – and sometimes made mistakes. And like most of us she tended to avoid people she felt she could not get through to.

With her special intuition for the individual behind the persona, Emilia Fogelklou showed a considerable empathy with people of the most differing kinds. To Elin Wägner: 'I know of few people whose difference to myself in peripheral matters I would *need* to such a degree as yours...'[31] And to KJ, the inimitable: 'We belong together at some point inside all the empirical, time, space, the "outer" meetings.'[32] Many have been surprised that they would match, KJ the brilliant, caustic critic and Emilia Fogelklou the passionate mystic: 'Holy is a fat word. You should never take it on your tongue without mustard,' is one of KJ's aphorisms. But in spite of her sceptical attitude to any organised religion, she could recognise a genuine and original spirit.

In KJ, Emilia for once found an intellectual equal and rebel like herself. She relished KJ's spirited irony and striking style. Both were in different ways searingly sensitive and were revolted by many contemporary trends. Appreciation was mutual. KJ wrote to Emilia: 'I love to see your fight and watch your restless flame rage against the sky. Fire and fruit-blossom is what you are, and before them I have the same sense of tenderness and almost painful worship. I don't want you tamer and more sensible and better adjusted.'[33] KJ also became Arnold's friend and helped Emilia edit and publish his literary remains.

Emilia and Arnold were resourceful and had contacts; they emanated a certain magnetism – people sought their advice and assistance, no visitor in need left without some form of help. Animals, too, came of their own accord, as Arnold had a strange ability to attract them. Emilia's speciality was people; she held a study circle in English for several years for anyone interested. They came faithfully, gardener as well as student. 'A cultural hearth in the forest' one of the locals called their home.[34]

Many of their old friends found their way to Lillstugan where Arnold and Emilia kept open house on Sundays. Emilia marvelled at how Arnold managed to listen interestedly to friends talking of children, successes and research trips abroad, all things that had been denied him. But Arnold's pleasure seemed genuine and generous. KJ and some friends returned from their visit to Greece – quite an expedition before everyone became air-borne. An Attic journey was what Emilia and Arnold had dreamt of making together. But when Emilia many years later went there, she was alone.

Friends from 'Infinity' also turned up and Arnold's brother Ernst sometimes brought another fiddle player and the 'book room' resounded with peasant dance tunes. Sisters, brothers, nieces, nephews dropped in. And tramps. One Sunday they happened to get 11 unexpected guests to dinner. Whether the beetroot burger or whatever they had to offer sufficed, the story does not tell.

During the first years of marriage there was renewed contact with Elin Wägner. Wägner had become editor of the weekly periodical *Tidevarvet* (The Era) of the Fogelstad Women's College and now she sought Emilia Fogelklou's contributions. Fogelklou was glad to write for this venture and in a long informative letter she opens her heart to Elin Wägner, where she describes her inner journey and the truth she feels she has found: 'You know, I'd so like to lumber you with the 'Cow', part II of *Medan gräset gror*, or actually just the part called 'Attempts at understanding'. It's not long. But in it is the essence of what I know and have experienced – I myself think that everything else I've written is just watered down compared with it.'[35]

In Elin Wägner, Emilia guessed that she had found a kindred spirit. The friendship would become life-long, nourished by mutual inspiration – and differences. They were direct opposites in many ways; Elin had a penchant for the large hats in fashion at the time and frequented beauty parlours, whereas Emilia never deviated from her modest dress. While Emilia let everything that happened within and outside her be irradiated by a kind of thorough rectitude, Elin had the bold velocity and amorality of the independent journalist.

Elin Wägner had a number of acclaimed novels behind her, she was also sought after as a freelance journalist, known for her skilful and spirited writing. Her style was often humorous with a light and apposite elegance which captivated – whereas Emilia Fogelklou struggled with a style rendered unwieldy in parts through her very sincerity, though her more successful efforts produced an 'exceedingly succinct' style, as one reviewer wrote.

Fogelklou's books were hard to sell. And yet! In spite of her keen awareness of failure there is a core of tenacious confidence: 'I, 46-year-old Emilia, without any success with my books, without any visible success to show, still have an invincible, irrefutable faith in being the bringer of something "new", if you like.'[36]

Yet another difference between the two friends was their way of involving themselves in contemporary life. Elin Wägner actively participated in meetings, debates and actions to stir public opinion, in a way which Emilia simply could not emulate. Emilia Fogelklou felt intensely part of her time, but she had to work from within a self-imposed isolation, away from all groups and parties, because she was *'unable to do otherwise'* for the integrity of her spirit.[37] Both intuitively and intellectually Fogelklou had the deepest mistrust of any kind of membership in organised work. Ever since she had been able to think independently she had observed how people were limited by the positions they adopted and then did not dare to move away from. 'Chalk lines' she calls the limits people drew up for themselves. Words like 'peace', 'women's liberation' become 'word-gods' round which 'the wheels of fanaticism run hot.'[38]

The peace movement and the Swedish defence question did actually become topics of heated political debate, dividing left from right. Being unable to take sides for either, Emilia Fogelklou often felt strangely left out by not participating:

> As far as I'm concerned I live in a strange isolated time ... The people's front is where there is noise and commotion. God's front is where nothing is yet heard, where things stir deep down. And therefore it is right and proper that I should gravitate from one front to the other. But maybe I only see it this way because I have never been able to find a public forum where I could serve with unsullied spirit.[39]

Staffan Björck has observed what this voluntary exile must have cost Fogelklou: 'She was the freebooter, in this there was a quality of being chosen, but also the seed of a great and tragic tiredness; never to feel the support of a routine, the security of what is generally accepted.'[40]

Their daily bread

Arnold and Emilia managed by hook or by crook to manoeuvre both illness and finances. To outsiders Arnold and Emilia appeared to manage well, very few knew how poor they really were. Emilia was a popular speaker, but as she mostly worked for idealistic organisations whose funds were small, the pay was scant. Added to that, some people took advantage of these selfless characters and Emilia would sometimes be asked to give lectures for free. In such situations she found it hard to control her irritation. A couple of times she was tempted to abscond from high principles and told

Arnold of the 'hair-raising' idea of giving talks just to earn money – somehow they must make ends meet! But even this didn't work. In one place her purse was stolen, in the other she was given expensive flowers instead of the usual pay. With a tearful smile she laid the exquisite bouquet on Arnold's bed when she came home. Blossoms, not bread.

This was the 'merry twenties' when a brief financial recovery meant that more people could afford a little luxury. The 'sinful' restaurant dance was introduced, skirts were shortened and the shingle hair cut was chic. On her visits to Stockholm and watching the world, Emilia could sometimes wonder about the justification of their life style, two highly educated people living so cut off and in such poverty.

At night she sometimes lay sleepless with worry about money, Arnold's illness and death biding by their side. But *every* time this occurred she had the strange experience that her thoughts must actually have woken Arnold next door with their sombre impact. She felt physically how great reviving waves of his spirit-presence swept over her body and soul. If her anxiety was too great to calm, he would come in quietly to sit by her side until all dark thoughts dissolved and they could both rest.

Tidevarvet's ever-burning lamp

Lectures and other things

> '*You can't smother your feelings, but you can educate them. Especially grief has an important function in all our lives.*'
> Vila och arbete p 45

Often Emilia managed to keep a balance between idealism and humiliating poverty with her down to earth sense of humour. She was a regular lecturer in the Psychology of Religion and Psychiatric

Health at the *Socialpolitiska institutet* in Stockholm from 1923 to 1928 and also gave at least one lecture-series per term at Jakobsberg folk high school close by. In her autobiography she reports on her activities in a cool and calm manner, but to her diary she admits her exhaustion: 'Yesterday 2 series ended. *Hoarse yesterday, but I managed!!*'[41] These lectures were published in a number of magazines and as collections of essays.[42]

All these public appearances might seem strange for a mystic to make. Emilia had thought that, except for her teaching, she preferably should write and rarely speak. But earning money was an issue and like many other mystics she believed in practical involvement. She was approaching fifty and had a rich store of experience to draw on, whether she addressed herself to factory worker, student or teacher. The human situation fascinated her down to the everyday details. The author of *Vila och arbete* is a strong and wise woman who talks common sense. Two of the talks had been addressed to housewives and here Fogelklou dares to question some of their tenderly nursed (mis)conceptions on topics like 'the care of the home' and 'the bringing up of children'. Emilia Fogelklou realised that women as well as men needed to reappraise old habits. Time has caught up with her message, and the reforms she suggested are now carried out. But if the details are no longer relevant, their spirit is still worth considering, e.g. 'The best thing is not to have *either* leisure *or* work, but to feel creative in your leisure and peace in the work itself.'[43]

Fogelklou constantly keeps in mind that it is the inner life that is the launching-pad for the outer. This lies at the heart of all her writing, whatever the subject. At home, the school desk or on the factory floor the same values apply: the active fresh response to the moment instead of sticking to old forms out of habit, compulsion or fear.

The year of crisis

> *'You see I have such a desire for life! I want to relish all I can of life's tremendous marvel'* letter 10.8.1925

But the summer days stood in painful contrast to Arnold's illness.

It had taken a turn for the worse – earlier that year a haemorrhage had seemed to herald the end. He needed a nurse 24-hours a day and Emilia was not allowed to see him. But one night they stole to a meeting. They sat looking at each other under the sky-light with the stars above. They felt a sharing, a kind of communion which they knew implied something new, a turning point: Arnold would live, however frail.

In the periods when he was not even allowed to whisper, he had discovered that he could make a noise like the barking of a dog without it hurting his throat. Soon the cottage resounded with happy 'bow-wows' as a welcome break to the silence. So the two balanced their days, but there were times when they nearly despaired:

> But we have both learnt that this takes too much strength from our real tasks, and when we feel tempted – me or Arno – we just say 'bow-wow' (!) And that means quite a lot. And then we laugh a bit – for we can laugh – and nod to each other and resume our work. But if I sit down to contemplate both sides of the narrow bridge of light, then all the dark waters come rushing to overwhelm me.[44]

They continued their striving with books that emphasised spiritual values. Despite his weakness Arnold worked hard on a book on Dante's life and times and Emilia, who had many claims on her time, also published the large, handsomely produced book for children, *Befriaren*, with 13 full-page illustrations by Fra Angelico from the life of Christ. Many years earlier Emilia had seen the originals in the St Marco Monastery, Florence, an experience that then outshone anything she had seen in London and Paris at that time. The book's title (The Liberator) testifies to Fogelklou's wish to free children's imagination rather than fetter it with doctrine. The purpose of all teaching was to help children find their own truth, not prescribe it for them.

After this book Emilia Fogelklou was planning a historical part for the middle school to be followed by a third with an 'ethically inspiring and liberating' content. Unfortunately they were never written. So much of her creative power was absorbed by lecturing and in caring for Arnold. It is hard for us to determine to what degree Emilia Fogelklou contributed to 'the spirit of the age' by the impact of her ideas and personality, but the lectures that found their way into print give an idea of her free and original spirit.

In her talks on education in 1926, she develops ideas from her earliest lectures of 1904; in the fact-ridden teaching that was fostered she saw that, at the same time, the imaginative elements were lost: 'the breathless listening is so often exchanged for practical and sensible observation. The consequence? An impoverished quality of life.'[45] Not until the end of the century were some spiritual and imaginative values allowed back into education and the balance begun to be redressed.

⁂

From 1927 on Arnold's health appeared slightly improved. They had spent three summers up at the small croft in Dalarna, a rural province renowned for its scenery. Arnold had managed to write several books. He could walk further than for years and felt he could manage library studies. Now his *Inferno* translation was ready for publishing and they were revising *Purgatorio* up to *Paradiso Terrestre* (Earthly Paradise). With Arnold feeling a little stronger they were both longing to take a more active part in society and, hoping for continued recovery, they planned a move to Stockholm. Now the time had come to leave their life in the forest for the wider world of the city. They more sensed than understood an ominous element in the political atmosphere where post-war optimism was already giving way to threatening tensions.

In Italy civil rights had been rescinded by Mussolini, all state organisations had become instruments of his power as 'capo del governo' and his 'black-shirts' exercised a rule of terror as military police. Hitler, who held Mussolini in great esteem, was soon to follow in his footsteps.

In Sweden, late but swift industrialisation had brought increasing prosperity. The socialist revolution was peacefully negotiated and implied a dramatically changed society. The concept of Sweden as a 'Home for the People' was launched in 1928, the Welfare state was hard on its heels, setting an example for the rest of Europe. But with this went a city and machine worship by the young generation which was not shared by Emilia Fogelklou; in her eyes the great mechanisation threatened to overtake human values.

For a couple of terms Emilia had lectured on 'Old and new spiritual knowledge'. The idea of studying religious practice in the light of modern psychiatry captivated her interest. To begin with the study seemed rewarding, like peeling pretence from a core of truth. Religion turned out to be a cover for much else. Her research was like turning over a stone. Strange clandestine little creatures scuttled away from the sudden light – could not stand to be seen for what they were: religious rite as flight from unpleasant duties, flight from life; pious practice and 'good deeds' seeded from insecurity or self-hatred. Jealousy, envy, sentimentality and a desire to show off could be other motivations for religious practice.

This was not edifying study. Fogelklou found it too caustic to continue and turned to a closely related area: megalomania – delusions of grandeur could occur in people with religious leanings. The English Quaker James Nayler was quoted as a typical case in the books she studied and her interest was aroused. But in Nayler she did not find the warped spirit she had expected, for closer study of his life yielded an image of a character whose high idealism had been travestied by a terrible fate. She found his last words, spoken on his death bed, to be one of the most marvellous spiritual expressions in the English language.

Fogelklou became captivated by this James Nayler, once a soldier in Cromwell's army, subsequently one of the important founder figures in the early days of Quakerism. She wanted to write his story and therefore had to plan a visit to Britain for source material. But first she must go on a lecture tour to get money for the move.

The move to Stockholm went well with help from friends. A

three-room flat where the high ceilings allowed space for Arnold's tall bookcases from Lund to come into their own again, filled with books from floor to ceiling in random order to start with. Arnold promised not to touch them until Emilia was back from her two week stay in London. Amongst other people there were two from 'Infinity', the close circle of friends from Arnold's student days, who were to keep an eye on him.

Emilia Fogelklou was well received in London, invited to stay with Mab Maynard (friend and translator of Fredrika Bremer), whose wit and sparkling intelligence brightened Emilia's labours at the archive in Friends House library. Every morning a letter from Arnold was waiting to spur her intense efforts, but reading between the lines Emilia knew that all was not well. If only she had been able to work night and day! On the ninth day she felt she must return, and exhausted after the toughest schedule of work that she had ever set herself, she came back to Arnold.

He looked ill and tired. At his proud 'I've all the shelves ready for your homecoming!' she was horrified and thought all sorts of rude words about bookcases. Books again! It was like some strange play-back of their earlier move. How pale he was. His heavy breathing!

Just before leaving Jakobsberg a friend had given them Thornton Wilder's *The Bridge of San Luis Rey*. The story of five people who die when a bridge collapses, ends:

> But soon we shall die and all memory of those five will have left the earth, and we ourselves shall be loved for a while and forgotten. But the love will have been enough; all those impulses of love return to the love that made them. Even memory is not necessary for love. There is a land of the living and a land of the dead, and the bridge is love, the only survival, the only meaning.

This image – a bridge of love – which Emilia so closely could identify herself with, came to have a special significance. It was the last book they read together, before Arnold too passed over the bridge.

They celebrated Christmas together, but Arnold's health was deteriorating. In order to pay the rent, Emilia had to concentrate on her book on Nayler. Arnold for his part was struggling with a commission for a Greek drama translation. Emilia herself felt unwell and overworked, constantly interrupted by visitors and the telephone. She became feverish and they had no help. How could she manage? Without her care Arnold needed a nurse. One night the crisis came to a head, when, sleepless, Emilia felt herself engulfed in the powers of darkness. Evil seeped through into the world that had been theirs, attacking and destroying. She had never experienced anything like this.

Then a warm wind came sweeping through doors and corridor, gently brushing her. Oh, how she recognised it! She knew where it came from. Able to rest, her fever receded and the next morning, 17th February, she went in to see Arnold. But one look told her that he had not long to live. Though unable to speak, his eyes and both hands reached out to Emilia, expressing all of his loving being.

> Mi felt as if he understood everything. He literally carried and lifted her... When he at last raised his head and chest and drew his last breath he had the most wonderful expression of amazed beatitude and a touching, incredible humility... He was not gone at all.[46]

Emilia still felt entirely surrounded by his presence. When she first stepped onto the pavement after his death, the thought flashed through her: 'Now Arnold and I can always go out walking together.'[47]

Grief and a sense of loss came later.

Kväkaren James Nayler (1929)

'...a passion play of intense suffering, a soul-stirring tragedy enacted before the whole people. But this is not the end. [...] we witness a human resurrection in the transfigured light of active peace, love and universality such as we dare dream of only somewhere beyond the gates of death.'

Kväkaren James Nayler p 15

One of the consequences of the Reformation was people's fight for religious freedom in seventeenth century England. They wanted to liberate themselves from the yoke of a patriarchal Church and government. Political freedom was a prerequisite for freedom of thought. The people rose up under Oliver Cromwell against the King and state religion: the civil war between Cromwell's Roundheads and the King's Cavaliers was a fact.

For a few years 1643–49 there was practically speaking religious freedom in the country. During this time of spiritual seeking the soldiers carried a gun on their shoulder and a Bible under their arm. Nayler was one who left his plough to volunteer for Cromwell's army. Every person sought his/her own truth about God. On street corners and in public houses religion was discussed with as much fervour as football results today. People were no longer content with being admonished by authority as to what to believe; now it was the ethical truth of each individual that counted.

The young Leicestershire villager George Fox had also got

caught up by the religious ferment. To him the gulf between people's faith and their life gaped wide. He found no satisfactory answer in churches, 'steeple houses' as he called them. After years of seeking he found clarity one night: it is within oneself that one has to seek truth. God is within every person, a concept he called the Light or the Seed. This was the message he took to people – and it still forms the core of Quaker faith. Fox's personality had extraordinary power over people and his words were said to fall like hammer blows.

The meeting between Fox and Nayler was a kindling of kindred spirits. Soon Nayler, with his clear intellect and gift of public speaking, stood beside Fox at the head of the new movement. It answered to a need of the time and grew with such strength that people in power felt threatened. Though entirely peaceful and non-political, the new Quaker sect was revolutionary in its popularity and refusal to bow to authority. The few years of religious tolerance were followed by persecution, imprisonment and in some cases capital punishment for dissenters. The quiet gatherings of Quakers were constantly broken up by officers of the law; meetings for worship were prohibited.

In contemporary accounts Nayler was called 'an arch heretic' and it was as such that Fogelklou began her study of him. She had no idea that she had stumbled on a great injustice and the source of the most serious conflict between two leaders of early Quaker history, briefly outlined here:

Nayler's personal charisma had caused some women to see in him an incarnation of Christ and they pursued him with excessive adulation. One of them even went to Fox to ask him to submit to Nayler's leadership, which germinated a conflict between them, as Fox thought the woman to have been sent by Nayler. This was a period of great darkness for Nayler. Ill and exhausted after a spell in prison he allowed himself to be led by these women, when in pouring rain he rode into Bristol where he was to speak. The women sought by their behaviour to make his entry resemble that of Jesus' into Jerusalem, calling 'Holy! Holy!' and spreading their cloaks before him. It was Nayler's only 'crime' – that he let it happen.

Parliament now had a welcome opportunity to pillory the unwanted Quaker movement. 'Blasphemy' was the greatest of sins. They brought Nayler to court and on the thinnest evidence sentenced him to public whipping and torture followed by three years in prison as a blasphemer against God. This obviously brought great dishonour to the Quakers – and Fox never forgave Nayler for having caused it.

By thorough study of source material and supported by partly unused material Fogelklou outlines a story that significantly differs from what was then generally accepted. She sketches Nayler's finely tuned and complex personality with the kind of rare inspiration that she earlier was able to summon for her portrait of Birgitta.

In contrast to Fox's immutably forthright character Nayler is a more listening and self-denying spirit, one of those 'who live at a quicker pace. They pass through transformations of destruction and new life. They travel further in undiscovered countries of the soul where the air is thinner and the dangers more rare than for most others. They are not in danger of stagnation. But they risk a tension strained to breaking point – and beyond. To rise again from being so broken not only requires a tremendous capacity for renewal but also a humility of spirit to accept the new premise among the wreckage in the wake of the storm.'[48]

Nayler bore all his suffering with the greatest patience and showed no bitterness. His last words are brimming with depth of spirit and light tolerance:

> There is a spirit which I feel, that delights to do no Evil, nor revenge any Wrong, but delights to endure all things, in hope to enjoy its own in the End: Its hope is to outlive all Wrath and Contention, and to weary out all Exaltation and Cruelty, or whatever is of a Nature contrary to itself.[49]

These words, now frequently quoted in Quaker circles, were also read at Elin Wägner's funeral in January 1949.

In spite of the pressure of time, the book seems well researched. But Nayler's suffering in some way also became Emilia's and Arnold's – in the many years' game of life and death they were defeated; when the book was finished Arnold lay dying.

Kväkaren James Nayler was published in an English translation[50] and was very well received and reviewed, though some Friends thought that Fogelklou's critical view of Fox was an exaggeration. The exceptionally positive reception in Britain was hardly matched by the Swedish. One could wonder if Fogelklou's writing in general would have been better understood if she had published in Britain, which was the case with Fredrika Bremer whose books sold far better in Britain than they did in Sweden.

Several years later Fogelklou tried to soften the impression of the blame on Fox in a Pendle Hill pamphlet *The Atonement of George Fox*, where she suggests that Fox sacrificed his personal power to establish a democratic system within Quakerism as amends for his implacable treatment of Nayler. Later biographers see no sign that Fox even regretted his action, which justifies Fogelklou's original point of view.

VI Forsaken (1929–1939)

> *'Nothing is so helplessly abandoned to the flux of time as literary remains. Like shells on the shore left by a wave that has travelled to another coast they lie there, these piles of diaries, letters, notes, cuttings… But maybe some listener can hear the music of the whole sea through some "sea shell".'* EF's preface to Arnold Norlind, *Skapande liv*, (1929, *Creative Life*)

When the first euphoria of feeling so close to Arnold after his death had evaporated, Emilia began to suffer the loss. In one letter she speaks of her grief like 'a girdle of ice',[1] in another of how she in a dream-like state saw Arnold with 'a coil of thorns round each foot'.[2] Life seemed no longer real. She lived in a vacuum on the periphery of existence, feeling superfluous. In the end she felt that she had failed – her love had not sufficed to keep Arnold alive. She read everything he had left and came to understand him even deeper than before, putting together two collections, one of essays and another of his diaries.

Then she wanted a change of scene. The world was full of things to discover. Most of all she would have liked to go to the India of Tagore and Gandhi who had just led the people in the 'salt march' to the sea in peaceful protest against the British salt monopoly.

But it turned out that America was more accessible and in September 1930 she was on her way to New York with a scholarship to study sociology and mental health.

America

The journey was a break. After many years in the forest she again breathed the sea air of her childhood. The cry of seagulls. The playful glitter of sunlight on water. Unreflecting timelessness.

Waiting in limbo, like an incubation. To what life would she be reborn, to what reality returned? Meetings with some solitary bird, an odd stranger. Fragments of conversations. 'Humility turns into intelligence. It gives you the ability to identify with the situations of others, not just your own', says the stranger. Emilia hears the words and understands they are spoken by a discerning person. But she no longer had an individual destiny, nor a 'situation'. How could she then identify with others?

In New York she found herself overwhelmed by the mass of students at International House. At first she was quite overcome: 'Imagine yourself a fly at some point in the Himalayas, who is trying to get an overview of the mountains – and you have my situation.'[3] She made the effort to involve herself and took part in the social life – at long last back in the larger world she had lived so distant from. 'But I have such a strong feeling in this huge, hurrying city that what people most need and long for is not one who *talks* to them, but one who *listens* to them. And this second level of work is to me the most important.'[4]

She had arrived the year after the great Wall Street bank crash and was very affected by what she witnessed: droves of jobless drifting down the streets, sleeping under bridges with their white collar in a paper bag, ready for the next morning's renewed job-hunt. People becoming mechanised in industry: 'no human being should have to do what a machine can do'. Fine. But how would you earn your living? Rush and redundancy. There seemed no pause between these twin factors.

In the world that Fogelklou encountered she felt as if a harsh wind had swept away the most sensitive elements in people, those that engendered silence and warmth: 'By the way this is a curious place. One is constantly kept busy. How people manage to have a bit of time to themselves and make little children I hardly understand.'[5] Everything was altogether so different from her life with Arnold.

A highlight in Chicago was the meeting with Thornton Wilder. He made a special impression on Emilia – perhaps because his book *The Bridge of San Luis Rey* was the last one she had read with Arnold. She found his observations on biography most inspiring and it affected her own approach to writing. He suggested a more impressionistic, less fact-ridden attitude to one's material than Emilia in her thoroughness had permitted herself. External details could become subordinate to an overall atmosphere. Fogelklou felt liberated and found that a more flexible method was not only allowed, but might actually give a more truthful picture. The question of the relativity of truth continued to occupy her. When she had started work on her book on Arnold she wrote to a friend: 'What is *order*? Everything doesn't happen in stripes and squares ... Administration is *orderly* if not always right. But the order of human arteries takes a different form and has another logic ... The *means* can destroy the *end*.'[6]

But while Emilia's daylight hours were spent in eager study of the world around her – from university to juvenile delinquency at Chicago Juvenile Court, she was haunted by an inner nocturnal reality, full of painful memories, questions: 'since Arnold now is gone all the things that I never noticed now come to avenge themselves: the constant uncertainty, money worries, the illness with the flow of phlegm, the childlessness and a thousand other things I never had the time to think about ... Old plans for 'real' work look at me like ghosts. For I share the fate of these American women, gifted and highly qualified who have come too late.'[7]

Was it all wrong, she asked herself – was that rainbow she had raised with Arnold above illness and poverty just a mirage, not worth its price? The only words that got through to Emilia at this time were: 'Why have you forsaken me?' She felt as abandoned by God as by Arnold.

'Reality scraped bare' she calls this time. She bitterly missed Arnold's spirit and the 'irradiated atmosphere' he created. She felt near to bursting with the dark humanity she had encountered. Now she struggled to regain an inner calm at the same time as sharing in the dismal destiny of mankind. Are there such resilient spirits, she asks, who can live without blinkers to the external world and yet remain open to the radiance that can penetrate and illuminate the past?

While in America she was offered a scholarship to study to be a psychiatrist. This seemed a worthwhile cause and Emilia seriously considered the offer. But it would also put a definite end to any literary ambition, and she declined. However testing the time in America, it had broken her isolation from the world.

Arriving home, exhausted but stimulated, Emilia thought she would devote herself to her neglected fiction writing. On two earlier occasions circumstances had forced her to give up such ideas – first when her sister Fej needed support, then when Arnold was ill. Now it happened a third time – her sister Nan, just widowed, had returned from Britain and stood without bed and board. Emilia felt duty bound to offer both.

She sighs in a letter: 'Now I have the whole summer packed with courses and lectures and I'm satisfied from the *earning* point of view. The surface of life is bubbling with trivialities, like the foam in the jam-making pot! But underneath! But inside!'[8]

If Fogelklou did not get the undisturbed peace that creative writing requires, she somehow found the time to sort through earlier pieces.

Den allra vanligaste människan

> 'I have ransacked my hoards. Most is for the fire. One or two things remained. And I have made a patchwork of the pieces here. If only it could warm some person.'

These words introduce a collection of articles, lectures and essays from 1917–31. The title of the book is significant: *Den allra vanligaste människan* (The most Ordinary Human Being). To 'be a human' was something Emilia Fogelklou prized above all else. Several critics have specially noted the first essay which begins 'There is no depth of human vice and aberration that does not reveal an eternal element – in distorted form.' Hans Larsson touches on the problem with the practical application of such an exceedingly tolerant attitude, but he also sees what a challenge it is and how inspiring it could be. Fogelklou clearly saw that an unequivocal respect for a person's own worth was a necessary first step in helping him/her take an own initiative to a better lifestyle.

'The most ordinary human being' as an ideal had turned up in diaries and letters ever since Fogelklou left Uppsala university, where she formulated the ideal: 'To strip oneself bare, dare to divest oneself of all knowledge, finery, understanding which is not genuine, and yet live with a burning intensity on the small island of life, where the ground is really firm under one's feet.' Her seeking had continued unremittingly since then. Earlier 'the most ordinary human' was to do with Emilia's personal attitude to life – later she widens the metaphor to include society as a whole: 'To me it seems that the same disarmament that is taking place in the armies is needed in preaching. I mean: vestments, showiness, sacraments – everything that corresponds to plumes, brass bands and such like. We need pure, naked, unadorned, disarmed humanity – otherwise we are nowhere near the gospel … "The most ordinary human being" is the goal – whereby I perhaps mean the same as the misused word humility.'[9]

Emilia Fogelklou had to continue finding sources of income. She filled her time with work, partly to assuage the grief and fill the void after Arnold, partly to earn a living for herself and the family. Emilia also felt duty bound to use her education and store of human knowledge. Here she was particularly qualified in the psychological field. She was in popular demand around the Scandinavian countries, lecturing on the psychology of religion and other related subjects to seminar students and professors, but her written output was still strangely overlooked.

From America she had written to a friend that she felt like the schoolgirl (over-age at 52!) who got left behind at her desk in life's classroom.[10] A sense of unreality invaded her. Outwardly all seemed well, but her inner person felt more and more like some robot. Was it grief? Illness? Or unfulfilment? She did not know. She probably did not want to live, as she had not found a new foothold since Arnold's death.

'One sees oneself in the mirror (if one happens to look that way) an old rough wrinkled face with drawn features. And one is full of ridiculous complexes and attitudes too. And those who don't look kindly from the inside, they see an old woman who hardly attracts. But that is all the more reason to love – *quand même* [anyhow], take an interest, *quand même*, make the effort. With open eyes, with self-humour. And compassion.'[11]

After the 'swinging twenties', the world crisis delivered its dark burden to Sweden too. The economic depression resulted in severe conflicts between employers and workers. Unemployment was at its worst during the winter of 1932-33 and there were violent clashes. A symbol of Sweden's new financial position of power had been the 'Match King' Ivar Kreuger, whose empire had crashed and whose suicide in 1932 spelt the ruin of thousands.

Hitler's frenzied voice on foreign radio stations was heard more frequently; his disquieting success presaged violence and ruthless usurpation of power. In January 1933 he was Germany's Vice Chancellor. Thinking people found the times deeply depressing. But the population at large was rather apathetic. They did not bother about what did not immediately affect them.

Emilia Fogelklou was painfully afflicted, 'I feel like a dead bit of trash ... I believe it must be the spiritual dead weight in the world adding to the pressure. People are desiccated by fear.'[12] All evil she observed was evidence of wrong attitudes that could never effectively be treated with action, only by the irradiation of prayer, she felt. Into silent worship she brought 'suffering humanity's strange path just now with sharpened bayonets and shredded thoughts of peace and brotherhood'.[13] When she wrote this letter she was at Woodbrooke, the Quaker College near Birmingham.

The Society of Friends (Quakers)

> '...my joining the Quakers is in line with an attitude I've always *had*' letter 22.9.1933

We know Emilia to have felt a natural affinity with Quakers ever since she from her school desk spontaneously declared her sympathy for George Fox. Now she had thoroughly studied early Quaker history with the Nayler biography and been deeply impressed. The Quakers' seeking to find God's presence in the present moment was exactly in line with her own striving:

> Ever since God became more real to me than I was to myself, eternity always became a *taskmaster* in relation to time. Eternity is the simple and natural thing, oh yes, but it is the taskmaster urging us to wrestle with the 'parenthesis' [life in the present] so that it might encompass eternity too.[14]

During her time at Birkagården Emilia Fogelklou had often wondered how contemporary democracy could rediscover its religious roots, so that life as a whole could be sacramental. In Quakerism she felt she had found an answer. Their organisation was not a theoretical construction, but had evolved organically on democratic lines. Men and women worked together on equal terms and carried equal responsibility. Fogelklou was attracted to their simple form of worship, she felt at home with their strong social involvement and care for others. It was like slipping into an already familiar and friendly family.

In November 1931 Emilia and Tove had applied for membership of the British Society of Friends as the Society did not yet exist in Sweden. They gathered for Sunday morning Meetings for Worship at Birkagården in Stockholm where the small group of 'seekers' slowly grew. When they felt strong enough they applied for state recognition as an independent Society; this was granted in 1935.

Emilia Fogelklou was invited as a fellow to Woodbrooke College in 1933–34. She felt honoured, especially as her book on Nayler had put Fox in a negative light. What should she now devote her attention to? Why not William Penn, another prominent figure in early Quakerism. But the person who sat down to write a biography of Penn was not at all the same as she who had captured Nayler's spirit with such empathy. Between them lay the loss of Arnold – and a sea-change.

Penn and Nayler were also very different individuals – Penn

prominent in the realm, adviser to the king and creator of his own state in America, would appeal to the extrovert side of Fogelklou, while the mystic in her would feel more identified with Nayler.

Four years had passed since Arnold's death, grief for him still affected Emilia's health with infections of various kinds and a huge weariness. All the same she was warmed by much kindness at Woodbrooke, where she even had a young secretary to assist her. So a well researched book on Penn was written in her native Swedish, translated into German, but unfortunately never into English.

William Penn

This book fills out the picture of the early history of Quakerism. Penn is a familiar figure to British readers, but not in Sweden. The Pennsylvanian peace treaty with the Indians in 1683 became historical. Penn's model state, founded on individual freedom and mutual responsibility, became a place of refuge for people from all over Europe who were persecuted for their faith. Fogelklou comments that the ideas in this unique democracy have not been put into practice since Penn's day: a de-militarised state. No arms – no armed aggression. Peace lasted for as long as this policy was maintained.

In the 1930s' growing international tension and with the spectre of another war looming, this book became a touchstone for many. One eminent critic wrote: '*William Penn* ... for me personally in 1935 – Hitler time! – became a Bible of democracy.'[15]

Fogelklou saw the Quaker way of working as a model for her time. In a talk given in 1947 she refers to the current debate in Sweden on 'the crisis of democracy' where the key issue was the question of how to combine political independence and the willingness to co-operate. Sweden felt squeezed between the great powers. Fogelklou cites the then overlooked and little known British philosopher John Macmurray's emphasis on an industrial democracy, i.e. education through local self-government with special attention paid to the democratic *quality* in the life of individuals and groups. Here Quakers could show the way with their centuries of striving for a poise between independence and co-operation.

Illness

'I don't remember the days of death. But I have been taken to countries other than where I was before' Resfärdig p 50

Back from Woodbrooke, Emilia Fogelklou filled her time with tasks of different kinds to earn her living. She forgot the strange sense of exhaustion in her busy work. In the autumn of 1934 she had a demanding schedule of lectures in psychology and mental health as assistant lecturer at the University of Stockholm, where she had rented a room. The cottage was not sold, but she preferred to live in the centre of town as simply as possible. 'Since I lost Arnold I've become a wild bird without goods and chattels. I can't keep the whole apparatus under control.'[16] But she was also feeling as if body and soul no longer belonged together, cut off from the 'organic' way of working which earlier she had shared with Arnold. In her rented room Emilia dreamt she was on a sea-bound ship, but it sailed in the wrong direction and she woke at her own anguished call for help.

Suddenly in the middle of a lecture she collapsed and was rushed to hospital. Double pneumonia cancelled all her engagements – death was very near. Weak and sleepless, she hung for weeks suspended in a high contraption rigged up for her as she could not lie flat. The night came when the oxygen failed to take effect and the family was sent for. Seeing their dear faces round her, Emilia then realised that her end had come. She felt such a surge of joy that now she would not need to bother with problems, the separation from Arnold and the whole palaver of life, that Death, the welcome guest, turned away. The paradox occurred that Emilia was so happy to die that she survived!

Life had just paused for a while, but slowly the pulse started beating again. Emilia Fogelklou must have had an extraordinary constitution, for she lived on for nearly forty more years! Fogelstad, which for so many years had been like a second home to her, now became her refuge where she was nursed for many months.

During her long convalescence one ailment followed another, her fever would not abate and Elisabeth Tamm arranged for a private nurse for her. She felt like a piece of driftwood, washed up on a friendly coast, a wreck, hardly alive but not yet dead.

When she eventually began to recover, she felt she needed to find anchorage for a life adrift, seek her spiritual wellspring. She realised that she was only at the beginning of her 'soul's journey'. She wanted to seek the connecting links between all her varied preoccupations in life. She needed to study her own history and for this purpose she travelled down to Skåne, as soon as she could, to look up the home of her maternal grandparents. As she began to look into family archives she found to her astonishment that her beloved grandmother was a child born out of wedlock to a young widow and the 23-year-old son of a neighbouring family. These humble origins would only have served to confirm Emilia's idea that religious quality is not dependent on social position and strengthened her regard for Hanna, her *mormor*.

Women, awake!

'A home, a bathing-place for one's spirit'
from a congratulatory telegram by EF to a Fogelstad anniversary

Fogelstads kvinnliga medborgarskola (Fogelstad School for Women Citizens) occupied a special place in Emilia Fogelklou's life as in society at large. Elisabeth Tamm, who instigated and financed the school, had opened her estate and manor house for this venture. Any woman from the age of twenty could attend free of charge. A large loft had been turned into a stylish hall for larger gatherings, with huge beams and deep window niches filled with flowers; it became a focal point in the lives of many women during the summer months that it was in use. Fogelstad represented a new phase of women's awareness – here they learned how to debate, how society functioned and what role they themselves could play in the making of the future. It was also a hotbed for new women's organisations working for peace, better working conditions and sexual equality.

In this laboratory for new ideas, male dominated society was scrutinised. Alternatives were debated and the discoveries of matriarchal societies provoked much discussion. As the ills of society were identified, the contours of the many-headed hydra began to emerge: misconceived and 'male' rationality, naïve machine-worship and not least, the continued destruction of the environment. This concern for the earth was voiced 30 years before Rachel Carson's *Silent Spring* (1962) and 50 years before general interest in conservation and ecology. Fogelstad at its best gave a tremendous sense of the interrelatedness of everything and the essential part women had to play in the world. The British Quaker Marion Fox visited: 'I didn't understand much. But I felt the spirit there.'[17] Fogelstad's importance for the education of Swedish women over several decades can hardly be overestimated.

Fogelklou was one of the main contributors, with lectures that 'swept across wide literary fields or gave a deep focus to topics on the philosophy of life'[18] according to one participant. As a speaker she made an 'unusual and brilliant impression: firm deep blue eyes, an intense rather deep voice, musically modulated on the Skåne dialect, a glowing insight'.[19]

With a glint of mischievous humour she anticipates the role women will play:

> In our time perhaps it won't be the knight setting the maiden free by killing the dragon? This time perhaps it will be the woman's turn to set the knight free from having to continue his life in a suit of armour – however up-to-date in its construction.[20]

This light irony was really the only way Emilia Fogelklou was able to approach the debate on women's rights. Any organised action was repellent to her:

> 'I feel so desperately disgusted at writing for women's rights ... yet I do know that I would a thousand times rather be a fearsome female than a lov-e-ly la-a-dy, if one should have to choose between two evils.'[21]

A main theme running through Fogelklou's mind this time was 'radiance' and 'radiation', words that combined many ideas and associations. She had always been interested in the natural sciences, now she studied the world of physics and was fascinated by the fact that the earth is surrounded by a light that the human eye cannot discern. 'Radiation' was also linked in her mind with the warm spot within her that appeared a few weeks after Arnold's death. She could not explain it physically, but sensed it as a source of strength more real and durable than many other physical experiences. It became a metaphor which followed her creatively for many years to find a final full expression in her collection of essays *Form och strålning*.

In spite of all her work, Emilia still felt as if she was just on the receiving end of life. In May 1935, whilst still bedridden with the aftermath of her illness, she received an offer of a three-year contract to lecture at Stockholm University on psychology and sociology. This gave her an important impetus for a renewed pursuit of her interests. She was in the special position of being a thoroughly schooled theologian, but remaining outside the Church. In this position she was able to make a unique contribution in bringing a spiritual dimension to psychology and psychiatry without leaning on the dogma of the state Church or its traditional religious language. Emilia Fogelklou was recognised as having cleared the way for the co-operation of theologians and humanists in the area of mental health. She had taken an active part in setting up the 'Swedish Society for Mental Health' in the early thirties and was a board member from its very beginning. When Poul Bjerre founded his Institute for Psychotherapy in Stockholm in 1940, Fogelklou was co-opted as a worker from the start, having already lectured and written widely on topics relating to mental health.

The long expected Spanish War broke out in 1936. All of Europe was involved, especially the intellectuals and of course Emilia Fogelklou too. She wanted to go as a relief worker, but was too poorly to travel. Instead she studied the Spanish mystics in the hope of bringing them to the people's attention as examples and encouragement for the people in Spain. She applied for means to study, but in spite of Archbishop Nathan Söderblom's warm recommendation she received no grant. There was an ardent interest in subjects like mental health, but matters of the spirit were put on the back burner.

Emilia never went to Spain, but kept many of her Spanish books for years.

Women's history

When Elin Wägner applied for membership in the Society of Friends, in the autumn of 1936, Emilia welcomed her warmly: 'Mother God will take you in her arms'. Emilia Fogelklou used this expression very sparingly, but significantly. For several years the two friends had been tracking the history of women, who appeared not to have existed in historical records.

By studying this unknown Woman's history the two friends tried to find an explanation for their own time and hoped to encourage women to pick up on a lost inheritance. The typical patriarchal society that had dominated so far could possibly be explained as a reaction to the supremacy of women in an earlier era. The friendship between Elin Wägner and Emilia deepened and intensified during some exciting years of research.

Fogelklou picked up a lead from Bachofen's *Das Mutterrecht* where he presents his theory that the original society was a matriarchal one. For a decade she had followed contemporary discussion of early matriarchal cultures – which she had fed into her lectures on family, sociology and psychology, ideas that she imparted to Elin, who swiftly kindled to them.

Their purpose was never to preach a possibly hypothetical matriarchal society, but to inspire women to a greater awareness of their unused powers. The idea was for women as for men to realise their own 'genius', an idea held by Fogelklou ever since she began to reflect on the matter: 'I think every person is intended to be a "genius", i.e. consciously, or rather superconsciously (in contrast to "subconsciously") *themselves*,' she had written during her Uppsala days.[22] This tallied well with the Quaker concept of each person fulfilling the divine element in them.

Emilia, who always greatly relished 'finding out about things' as she would say, often travelled down to the very busy Elin in the country and summarised books for her on matriarchal cults, fertility goddesses and old myths. All was grist to the mill for new thoughts relating to the contribution women might make in the contemporary situation; the atmosphere in Europe was threatening. The German Quaker Yearly Meeting that Fogelklou attended in the summer of 1938 was held under police surveillance.

Academic adventure

'"May I have my daily courage to commit some peccadillo", as KJ used to say.' Resfärdig p 116

Returning from the German Yearly Meeting Emilia Fogelklou found a letter from a friend waiting for her, regarding a new chair in the History of Religion with Psychology of Religion at Uppsala. He urged her to apply – Uppsala had historians, but none with her expertise in the psychology of religion. She sought the advice of three trusted professional friends, who all supported the idea, though one suggested she should publish something on a subject outside the history of Christianity, which up till now had been her main area of study. The treatise on which she based her application was thus on 'Religious practice amongst Swedish women before the introduction of Christianity'. She could use some of her research on the matriarchal society and apply a different angle. This subject was virgin ground. She had only three months in which to write her specimen paper, enough time to introduce areas of research and lines of approach but too little to follow them up scientifically. She spent some wonderfully happy and undisturbed working weeks in Lillstugan, the cottage, while the farmers were gathering the harvest from the fields around. But the idyll was disturbed by news of the Jewish pogroms on Kristallnacht, 10 November 1938. Her international contacts brought everything so close; she identified painfully with the displaced Jews. But she finished on time and handed in her papers later that month.

The whole adventure ended worse than she could have

expected. Because in terms of the chair the Psychology of Religion was subordinate to the History of Religion, she not only lost the chair, but was declared unqualified for it. This outcome was made public by the press.

Pendle Hill, summer 1939
'There was an unusual and natural ease between students and lecturers...' Resfärdig p 127

At the time of this ignominy Emilia Fogelklou was again visiting America giving a series of lectures on 'Individualism and Community life amongst seventeenth century Friends' at Pendle Hill, the Quaker college in Wallingford, Pennsylvania. The writers Aldous Huxley and Christopher Isherwood had left just before she arrived. During the summer of 1939 there were artists, doctors and a dance company staying there. With the hosts Anna and Howard Brinton's learned and generous company, people from almost all over the world met at dinner or over iced lemon tea. Fogelklou absorbed everything, including what Emily Parker, her friend from Woodbrooke, reported about the heavy relief work in Spain – which Emilia had missed through ill health.

All these impressions turned the Pendle Hill stay into a colourful experience of intellectual stimuli, meeting people and discovering old Quaker history. They visited the eighteenth century home of John Woolman, staunch champion of the slaves. For Emilia the visit was imbued with the presence of Arnold in her mind, as she had always thought him of John Woolman's ilk.

Summer courses were led by Professor Douglas Steere, well known in Sweden and a von Hügel specialist, Emilia's treasured friend from the Olaus Petri scholarship journey. After the end of the course Emilia went with the Brintons to different depressed areas, Western Pennsylvania, Tennessee and Michigan. Here work was scarce and Quakers had initiated student camps run on similar lines to the 'settlement' idea with the young sharing the redundant workers' lot – this hands-on experience was different from theory! They lived, tasted, felt hopelessness and poverty. And took part in creating new enterprises and small factories. Being in the young peoples' company had a liberating and positive effect on Emilia and the experience of these work-camps was to prove very useful in Sweden.

But the boat on its homeward bound journey was met by the news of Germany's invasion of Poland on 1st September.

The second World War had broken out.

VII Renewed Endeavour (1939–1972)

Germany, autumn 1939
*'...people blindly approaching the yawning abyss....
They see no precipice'* Resfärdig p 150

Everything shrank into insignificance compared with the great conflagration taking place and Emilia Fogelklou forgot her private troubles as she immediately set out to where she could be of use, in the small office in Hamburg set up for Quaker relief work. Quakers were the only organisation who had permission to help Jewish families across the border to other countries, thanks to the efforts of Rufus Jones, the American historian. During November 1939 Fogelklou took part in the work at the office at Louis-Ferdinand Strasse in Berlin, a rescue action that was continued until 1942.

When Emilia had gone to the Hague in 1915 she had watched singing soldiers bedecked with flowers seen off on departing trains. Now no song was heard, there were no flowers and nobody waved farewell. The women stifled their despair – what was the point of all this, the war devouring husbands, sons. 'Where does this lead? Are we facing the destruction of humanity? How can suffering be transformed into creativity?' were questions put to Fogelklou.

In December Finland was also drawn into the war through the Soviet Union's invasion of that country. The risk that Sweden would be invaded was imminent. Fogelklou was forced to leave her work and return home.

At home in Sweden
When the Finnish winter war of 1939–40 began with the Russian bombing of Helsinki, the whole world – with arms folded –

expected Finland to fall within weeks. Finland was given little help against the aggressor, many times larger. But the Finnish people made an incredibly tough and brave stand, helped by Swedish volunteers, and managed to hold out for quite some time.

'What is happening affects me physically, it stifles me, I can't work, I've dried up...'[1] The black-out gloom of war across Europe corresponded to Emilia Fogelklou's own curtained destiny. The dishonour of her academic failure was threatening to destroy her just as the war was disintegrating the world around her. She felt 'dismissed and dead in official Sweden'[2] and struggled inwardly for a long time to overcome her despair and bitterness. She had however been too hard hit ever to get over it completely – she felt as if she had been failed in the very area she had made her own. Perhaps her experience in early childhood and youth increased her burden of failure: the sense that she had been chosen for a purpose since childhood now seemed held up to public ridicule. KJ's early prediction that the rare Emilia Fogelklou would 'be stoned or crucified in some way, one of these days' had found its gloomy fulfilment.[3]

The disqualification also had long after-effects of a purely practical nature, when the demand for her lectures dried up and she was not offered any properly paid qualified work. She found it extremely hard to make ends meet for a number of years to come. She started study circles free of charge and gave a series of talks on the radio. Outwardly her stress was not seen; the work kept her going.

K.B. Westman put Emilia Fogelklou's name forward for an honorary doctorate at the theological faculty of Uppsala, which she accepted after some hesitation. Maybe it smacked a little of a consolation prize to her sensitive pride. She was the first woman in Sweden to receive this honour in 1941.

Emilia Fogelklou now entered a difficult period. How should she reach out to people with the message which she still felt was hers and unique? She knew she had an intuitive insight into hidden connections under the simmering surface of life, but without being able to impart her vision so that people could understand.

Maybe Elin Wägner could come to her aid? Emilia admired her for her elegance, clarity and engaging style. Perhaps Elin could help Ili, her friend and sister, to become better known by writing about her? Fogelklou had done the same for others on several occasions. But Wägner had her own problems, overwhelmed with work, unfinished writing and delicate health. She also found Fogelklou a far too multi-faceted person to write about. She did not fully realise how keenly Emilia desired her help – and prevaricated.

Maybe the two friends were too close. It was a time of trial for them both. Emilia again felt displaced and rejected by her friend's seeming unwillingness to champion her; Emilia felt herself a failure: 'I would so like to see where I lost my way. For I set out with a great sureness and a purpose. And here I lie so helpless, cut down from the loom of life.'[4]

Elin, for her part, was caving in under the expectations placed on her. She felt it would be 'child's play' to write a biography of Selma Lagerlöf (her next projected work) compared to writing on Emilia Fogelklou: 'Because in writing about you, one has to dare enter into all the areas where you have worked. One has to describe your particular and remarkable way so people understand it.'[5] Their friendship recovered as soon as they became fully aware of each other's situation and in the new year of 1941 they were co-operating again. This was the year they both published important books which in different ways reflect their research into women's history, Wägner's *Väckarklocka* (Alarm clock) and Fogelklou's *Bortom Birgitta* (Beyond Birgitta).

Bortom Birgitta

'She aimed at tracking a path that she thought would encourage other people's continued research.'
Resfärdig p 115

Many people regarded this book, the result of Fogelklou's research for the abortive attempt at an academic career, as amongst the best she had written. It is a collection of studies of early societies introduced by a thorough overview of up-to-date research on early matriarchal communities, linking them with the age of the thirteenth century Swedish Saint. Based on original documents, Fogelklou now fills out the picture of Birgitta she had drawn in 1919. Woman's strong position at the time when Birgitta lived could be traces of an old cult of woman, which lingered in the inherited concepts of the medieval mind.

As before it is Fogelklou's ability in close reading of original documents that yields fresh material. Her ideas tumble out with evident enthusiasm for her subject; the style is clear and concentrated. By bringing these early pre-Christian societies to light, in which women had been able to make such a significant contribution, Emilia Fogelklou was hoping to provide an example for women of the war-generation to emulate.

One eminent critic recognised the value of *Bortom Birgitta* and saw Fogelklou as 'a woman scholar with the clearest mind and the finest heart within the modern Swedish women's movement.'[6] But others were dismissive or indifferent. Both Wägner and Fogelklou had set out to rouse women's awareness in a world aflame with war. *Väckarklocka*, especially, was an impassioned plea for women to take action for the earth and for peace. They did not respond. Neither book seemed to make much impression on women or men numbed by the enormity of the war-machine.

Emilia was used to adversity and took the long view; she knew that 'deep reactions take their time'.[7] But Elin saw for the moment her hopes ground to dust. Even Emilia Fogelklou's patience was strained after a year of no response: 'I see minute by minute how important "our" new feminine awareness is, but oh, how little sympathy and understanding [there is]. Our work just seems to drop as through a trap door, no one even takes the trouble to review it – sheer indifference. But one has to plod on all the same. "Celà aussi passera" [This also will pass].'[8]

The two friends did not doubt the long-term importance of their work, however. They knew they were writing for future generations.

Now they were free to turn to other fields – both had projects waiting. Elin Wägner had been commissioned to write a biography on Selma Lagerlöf and Emilia Fogelklou had been planning a book about Arnold ever since his death. Now they could settle down to their respective tasks.

Relief work

The mass murder of war did not seem to have an end. 1942 came – and still there was no peace. Sweden's position as the only Scandinavian country outside the war meant that it was a refuge for many. Denmark had been occupied since early 1940, soon followed by the invasion of Norway. The flow of refugees was constantly growing. One of them was Wolfgang Sonntag, who had fled to Norway and from there had to find safety in Sweden. Here he was amazed at young people's indifference to the war – they had unique opportunities in an unoccupied country! Wolfgang felt that he must rouse this apathetic young humanity to a sense of responsibility and fellowship with others of their age in warstricken countries. Young and burning with enthusiasm for creating a new kind of peaceful civil service he wanted to enlist Emilia's support. Wolfgang's enthusiasm was infectious – and tiresome, as he had no patience with the slow moving bureaucracy of building an organisation.

Emilia Fogelklou, now in her sixties, had a fund of knowledge from American work camps and Quaker relief work abroad, apart from gathered knowledge of human nature acquired during a long and hard-working life. The idea of people working together, learning tolerance in this time of crisis, appealed to her. Wolfgang presented his ideas at the Quaker Yearly Meeting in 1942, and from then stems the beginnings of IAL (*Internationella arbetslag*, International Work Camps). Emilia promised her

Hitler's dream – Europe's nightmare
Le Rive, Paris 1939

help when she had time.

The first task for the new organisation soon presented itself: in December 1943 a wave of Danish refugees flooded into southern Sweden and some were siphoned off to an empty dilapidated mansion in the middle of a forest. Nearby was also a sheep farm where some could find work. One had to quickly find things to occupy these uprooted people who had ended up in the forest just over Christmas. They started making furniture and straw decorations on a large scale. Emilia was busy all day long in talks and discussions – the stress and anxiety amongst the refugees was considerable. Those who were not busy with the sheep she tried to involve in some study, which was difficult as there were hardly any books. But with humour and imagination a lot could be achieved. Emilia Fogelklou was in her element.

One member of a work camp recalls her as 'beyond all compare; she spared no time and effort. What a fountain of knowledge in psychology and sociology! What alertness in body and soul, what an infectious indomitable quality she emanated when she – at 66 – got lost running through the woods with us on the way home from some biodynamic meeting in the village!'[9]

Another participant remembers Emilia's very presence as a calming influence, when visiting a team building roads in Småland: 'We were talking eagerly and naïvely of how we were going to change the world. Ili sat with us one evening, listening to our cocksure ideas, picking up a sentence sometimes, turning it over. Quietly, never superior but with clarity and intelligence. I admired her enormously. Had such a strong impression of the light in her.'[10]

Arnold

> 'I'm always longing – as though for paradise – to live in the country and write in peace...' letter 20.1.1944

How Emilia Fogelklou with all her involvement in the practical 'outer' world managed to find time to gather herself for such an inwardly listening work as *Arnold* is one of the many riddles of which her life is so full. Her life was as usual brimming with people and business that needed urgent attention. Fogelklou admits in a letter that consequently her writing is slow, proceeding 'like a louse on a tarred stick', (as they'd say in Skåne). Yet the 'Woe of the world', as she called it, was maybe also a spur to writing this story of a love which has no equal in Swedish literature, 'The most important reason for publishing such a book now, is perhaps its untimeliness', Fogelklou writes in the preface. The book is a celebration of a lifelong life of the spirit, self-denial and love: Fogelklou's tribute to the unique quality of Arnold and their marriage.

She had set herself a daunting task and one in which she felt she would inevitably fail: 'It is difficult to write about spiritual experience. It is not measured according to its literary expression. It is like things from the depth of the sea, which lose their true nature when hauled up on dry land. The seaweed turns into a green streak, or the kelp to a brown rag; the jellyfish becomes a little dead slime.'[11] But through the lyricism of her prose and felicitous metaphors, Fogelklou has managed to afford us a glimpse of this elusive inner world. This book became her greatest success with both public and critics.

The fact that Emilia herself had to be both a nurse and busy bread-winner for seven-and-a-half years, hardly figures in the story – she never saw herself in that light. Life with Arnold was a privilege – his suffering was also hers. This is Martin Buber's 'I – Thou' spirituality turned into practice. But privately, in a letter to a friend, Emilia has also admitted what it took: '… yet these seven years were not *only* a sinecure for me. I made tremendous efforts, but as a mountain walker in clear air can walk so much further than otherwise, so it was for me, for as long as I could accompany Arnold uphill.'[12]

The book found an audience. It inspired two authors – one to write a radio play in which he turns against the currently trendy primitivism in 'our clumsy time which only believes in the meeting of bodies'. Another writer wanted to base his own approach to a beloved on *Arnold*, as, he says, 'it describes how two people erotically and spiritually interweave their personalities to form a life together.'[13]

In spite of the war Emilia Fogelklou had managed to get a visa from December 1944 until February 1945 for travelling to Britain to study questions of rebuilding, which must have seemed urgent enough as she picked her way through the rubble that had been London. But her mind was also set on restoring other aspects of the shattered world, and as such her visit was rewarding in that it resulted in many lectures, articles and reports on the situation. After coming home Emilia was working tirelessly with refugees and work camps, often feeling worn down and exhausted. In spite of the 1945 peace the stream of refugees did not seem to abate. She worked with different groups in all the Scandinavian countries and particularly with Douglas Steere in Finland.

As soon as was practicable, IAL arranged work camps in Hamburg, then a pile of ruins. As expected it was harder to create a sense of fellowship, not many came to the silent gathering at the beginning of the day. But they could build barracks with the German young people, mend shoes and organise day care for the street children. Fogelklou found herself stretched to her limits, which actually suited her best and her diary laconically records 'an almost constant inner joy, right through the thickening darkness out there.'[14]

Högfors

> *'Here were still waters and deep silent forests. But here was also a friendly centre...'* Resfärdig p 207

At an interval in her rebuilding work, Emilia Fogelklou went to see her friend Florrie Hamilton at Högfors, the eighteenth century manor house at Högfors Iron Works, surrounded by a park with a gazebo and a charming wooden bridge over the pond. Florrie had devoted her life to making the manor a focal point and to keeping alive the tradition of the manor house culture of a past age. She received refugees, guests from far and wide and arranged soirées for the locals. Youngsters saw her as the good fairy at Högfors, organising games and frolics. She cultivated her large vegetable garden according to the biodynamic ideas that Elisabeth Tamm and Elin Wägner had so much at heart.

During her walks in the park Emilia saw an inviting little cottage, uninhabited. The war was over and she was now 68 years old. Time to withdraw, she felt. She imagined going into silence like the Tibetans, away from the world. Encouraged by Florrie, she decided to move there; dinner could be taken at the manor. '*Now I am* a hermit!'[15] she exclaims in a letter to a friend after her move. But Emilia soon found that this was a statement which required some modification. Her presence at Högfors acted as a magnet and people took advantage of Emilia Fogelklou's natural hospitality. KJ is mercilessly mirthful at Emilia's report on her situation:

> The description of your predicament was touching but also tragicomic. Fancy, we said, there Klou has taken herself off into the country with all her chattels so as to be rid of hangers-on and enjoy the peace of mind and work of a hermit, and then it turns out that she has immediately opened a hostelry under precarious circumstances! We fear that the place soon will be notorious and attract people like flies.[16]

This fear was well founded. To begin with Emilia tried to cook for her guests, but soon arrangements were made for her visitors to stay for a brief spell at the manor house. KJ wondered about the wisdom of the move: 'I do somewhat doubt that she *really* is happy in her new home. Perhaps she is feeling rather lost in the world since Arnold left it.'[17] This was a conjecture with some justification. Emilia Fogelklou's self-discipline kept her going with a swim at 7.30 every morning and long walks in the forest. But there were pale winter days when she walked alone with no distraction from her self-examining spirit. Nature could take on an ominous physiognomy. the naked birch became 'a corpse of summer' and the jagged silhouette of the pine forest seemed to bite the sky to the anguished howl of the Högfors iron works. Maybe she associated these reactions with the inevitable existential anguish that Kierkegaard had written of. She had all her life tried to shoulder her individual responsibility in poverty and privation. To what purpose?

So much knowledge of human nature that she had gleaned. All the incredible 'feasting and famine' she had shared with people in their lives, while she herself had not made a real contribution, but remained a Jack of all trades. But then she smiled at her pretensions: why should she imagine herself other than 'the most ordinary human being'?

Yet she had things she wanted to say.

> When we think that life 'passes us by', it is an illusion. It is just that we latch on to external matters, material things. We are unaware of the fact that every joy and pleasure, sorrow or strife, every person, animal or object, every discovery, is a call to us, which we actually always respond to even when we do nothing. World events as well as everyday ones quite simply come to *test* us: How do you react to this? Do you want to or don't you? Do you know or not? Do you care about seeing, knowing, wishing to, responding?[18]

One seems to hear echoes of Kierkegaard's and Martin Buber's urgent questions, relevant for all times.

Pioneer again

Emilia Fogelklou's active interest in people could not be kept down for long. Could all her study and long experience of mental health and psychology not be made use of out in the country too? Emilia Fogelklou was approaching her seventies but was still hale and hearty. She discussed the matter with the district medical officer and soon started a counselling clinic once a week in each of two nearby villages. To begin with she had only few clients, but soon they came in numbers with their confidences and problems. She shared so much human woe. In her diary she notes 'A rare joy through this listening, despite everything.'[19] To her it was a practical application of an attitude she had expressed many years before:

> If one does not put on blinkers when saying 'God', but dares to honour and look every ounce of reality, however profanely attired, straight in the eye, then one will find a wonderful concord in the apparently so different halves of knowledge, the medico psychological and the old mystic. 'With all mind and might' – not *only* the intellectual, not *only* the emotional – one can then seek and find God-given aptitudes in place of one's soul's decrepitudes, so that one after another is transformed from inhibition to creative power, from the subconscious to the God-conscious.[20]

In order to work towards this goal Fogelklou realised she must intercede for her clients with prayer as an inner radiation for the person seeking relief. She found yet another link between psychoanalysis and religion: 'analysis should after all lead to a veneration for life.'[21]

Soon official recognition came: in 1947 the Swedish Society for Mental Health wanted her to start a counselling service in Västerås with consulting hours twice a week. This was the first of its kind in the country. Fogelklou promised to start as soon as she returned from the summer's rebuilding work in Hamburg with IAL. In her biography she humbly writes that she could not tell if her work had any lasting value for her clients. All letters and other documents relating to this counselling work have been destroyed in accordance with Fogelklou's strictly observed professional confidentiality and we therefore do not have the necessary evidence. But the fact that she tells of using not only all her energy, but also all she had ever learnt, is a sign of a total commitment. All her strength was spent during the counselling sessions, embracing the whole situation and holding the person from within. She was quite exhausted at the end of a work session, even physically in her muscles and nerves.

Quaker ways

Emilia Fogelklou's work for Quakers did not cease. The American Friend Douglas V. Steere recalls a meeting in 1947 with a group of Swedish Friends, shattered by the sudden death of Per Sundberg, educator and peace worker. Per had visited Germany several times since war ended and had seen the exhausted, undernourished and demoralised leaders for the rebuilding of Germany. Per had suggested a plan whereby some twenty of these people would be invited as guests of the Swedish Quakers for a month, with an equal number of leading workers from Scandinavia, France, Swizerland, Britain and the USA to meet with them during one week of their stay, to make them feel totally accepted in the common cause of rebuilding.

It was a wonderful idea. But the project was elaborate and expensive, in that it required a number of exit and transit permits as well as food ration allowances and all the costs to be met.

> I knew that the rational judgement of the small group of Swedish Friends who had gathered was that, without Per Sundberg's leadership in carrying the central burden of what had to be done, they were quite unequal to the task of undertaking the concern ... and there seemed unity in the wisdom of a negative response. ... Emilia Fogelklou rose and ... like a prophet of old, she went on to say that there had come to her in the silence a wave of assurance that they must not fail Per's concern, that strength would be given them to carry it out. ... Within a few minutes three persons had offered their services to form a small secretariat to cover the principal tasks, and all had pledged themselves to assist as they could.[22]

Three months later the German guests were in Sweden and their counterparts from Western countries arrived for the international conference of goodwill that Per Sundberg had envisaged.

Emilia Fogelklou became increasingly known and respected as a leading personality of her day. Her persistent efforts with lecturing, relief work and publication had at last made an impression. Even if her writing did not reach a wide audience, there were friends who wanted to save certain essays from books, now out of print. One of them made a selection of 15 essays from the past under the name of *Ljus finns ändå* with the new addition of a recent radio broadcast that Emilia Fogelklou had made, 'Between the Great Powers'.

'Perhaps we believe that we want to get away from the methods of war. But how we allow ourselves to be pulled along, resigned slaves of routine. There are situations when people who call themselves Christians dread the words "Love your enemies".'[23] Her demand for individual effort in this time of the Cold War has not abated: 'Prayer and contemplation – this means of education for our subconscious which is so pushed out of the way in the relentless present – should always be practised alongside studies and work. It claims *all* of us, not just a part.'[24] The book was respectfully received, but largely ignored by the general public.

The two friends Elin and Ili felt that their writing was unwanted, frozen out by the chilly cultural climate, still dominated by rational attitudes where the spiritual element had no place.

Emilia Fogelklou stayed at Högfors from 1946 to 1951. During this time she made several lecture tours and Quaker-connected visits to all the Scandinavian countries, several times to Finland where Douglas V. Steere particularly remembers a small international conference:

> Early in 1948, I wrote to ask her to join with five other Friends ... in Finland with [two other organisations] to see if and how we could be led to perpetuate the memorable experience of true Christian community

that we had known working together during the
three years of the Quaker Relief Project in Finland.
She replied that publishers' deadlines and urgent
work she was involved in would keep her from being
able to accept. I wrote her at once that I more than
understood and had hesitated even to ask her,
knowing how pressed she was. A week later I had a
letter from her saying that all the obstacles to her
acceptance still remained, but that it had come clearly
to her that she must accept. In Finland, at this gathering, she helped us to arrive at a decision to establish
Viitakivi, the Finnish International High School that
has flourished in the years that have followed. [25]

A small international conference was held at Viitakivi in 1948 on the same lines as those held at Viggbyholm: practising a spirit of community in living with others. Participants were given a first hand report on India's declaration of independence: the British Quaker Horace Alexander's description of his time with Gandhi during the dramatic days in August when Hindus and Muslims were raging against each other.

Barhuvad

Apart from all outward activites the Högfors years were also a time of reflection and retrospection. Fogelklou gathered memories and material for *Barhuvad,* the story of her life before meeting Arnold. Her friend Elin Wägner had encouraged her in the enterprise:

> Your experiences as a woman student from the turn
> of the century and onwards is a piece of feminine
> history that no one has experienced or can describe
> like you ... You have no excuse. At Högfors you have
> both telephone service and angel service. You are not
> worn out in either body or soul. Your spirit is
> sprightly. You haven't a grey hair ...[26]

This letter, written on Emilia Fogelklou's 70th birthday was actually never sent, but presumably Elin also persuaded her in conversation. Or else it was just in the air, for a month later Emilia writes to her friend that she feels 'duty bound to write some sort of autobiography, which I flee from and yet desire to do.'[27] What was Fogelklou's purpose in writing her life story? It certainly was not self glorification. There was something that even late in life she still felt the need to express, something people still had no ear for, which in book after book she tried to formulate without really being heard. So she must try again. In a letter to Elin Wägner in January 1944 her thoughts return to her 'two cows', *Medan gräset gror I & II* (1911), which she felt contained the core of what she had to say: 'What I try to express there is also *behind* all my other output, whether written in a hurry or sought out slowly with a dowsing rod. But I have all my life had the role of a breadwinner to fulfil, so there hasn't been much time to *really write* (or am I just saying this? – have I been too tempted by "life with its seductive banality" to write? I think that after my journey to England I'll have the *right* to write a kind of autobiography.'

A quote from an earlier play for children, the only one we know by Fogelklou, *Drömtydaren* might give a clue. Jacob has this to say:

> 'Only he who smiling bears the scorn and taunting
> has the *right* and *duty* to give the world his dreaming.'[28]

A mystic at heart, and frequently scorned by the world, Fogelklou identified closely with Jacob, the dreamer. She thought it right for her to write her story, for the sake of the truth she had tried to follow. She felt she owed it to herself, and in that sense it was her duty. The important thing is the mission that carries her – and it also carries the narrative, illuminating the writing from within. The Revelation of Reality dazzles the reader with a reflection of that light that struck her as a 23-year-old, and by which everything she had ever learned and lived since then had been irradiated. And when she scrutinises the world and its values in the light of this revelation, the reader encounters a mind with a strikingly fresh approach. The essence discovered behind appearances often runs counter to received concepts.

E. Hj. Linder, Professor of Literature and figurehead for a more open approach to literary criticism, observes that the book has an aura. Not so much for the picture of the time or the people passing by, but because Emilia Fogelklou is a burning spirit. One single great experience has dominated her life ... and the reader realises that it penetrates every page that follows. How often is one given such books to read? It is a religious and psychological document and a guide for those who stumble in the same direction without being granted the same intense certainty.[29]

According to him, Fogelklou is 'in contact with the best and most religious life of our time' and the study of her as a person and a writer can teach us something of what religion is.

Journey to classical countries

1951 – ISRAEL

All her life Emilia Fogelklou had wanted to explore the two countries she saw as the cradle of Western civilisation – Israel and Greece. The Biblical Israel seemed to hold messages for her own time. Now at last she could walk this holy ground and at the same time visit the new Israeli state in its infancy. She was to find both good and bad fairies at its cradle.

With unerring intuition – or was it just luck – Fogelklou makes contact with the most important people in the new state. Hugo Bergman is the person who, in his way, corresponds to what von Hügel meant during Emilia's Olaus Petri journey. Bergman has just arrived at a university where the shelves are still empty of books. He and Fogelklou have long talks together. He fears that the Jewish state will not be able to retain its character: 'For a politicised people there is a danger in "becoming like all others" and casting off one's uniqueness ... there is no other way than the crystallisation round the plumb line.'[30] By which he implied a gathering of spiritual strength that goes deeper and is more powerful than verbal expression.

Emilia Fogelklou saw the Israeli situation as an image for the whole western world in a nutshell. Bergman's 'plumb line' is something all civilisation must centre on in the spirit of Eckhart: 'we must crack the shell for the sake of the core!' Outer divisions, walls, borders must be cleared away for a new common humanity from the most personal relationships to general and public ones.

But before Emilia left Israel the first shots were fired after the cease-fire on the Jordanian border, the beginning of the territorial conflict that is still unresolved.

GREECE

Though the two countries share the Mediterranean, Emilia Fogelklou found the sea between Israel and Greece like the deepest divide. The Hellenic morning sun dawned on a world without the slightest apparent connection with the one she left. The carefree kindness of the Greeks carried no sign of the great suffering they had just been through. In Israel Emilia Fogelklou had constantly sensed a latent conflict; here people lived in a more relaxed manner. The woman in the poor home with only tin pots for cooking bade her welcome with the dignity of a queen.

But all urgent questions cease when she visits Delphi. This is where she and Arnold had wanted to go together. And now she is here at last – without him. But she does not feel lonely: Arnold is at her side. The two spend the day in natural and joyful companionship, visiting the home of the oracle, bursting with youthful exuberance and energy. Emilia's 72-year-old body felt not a trace of tiredness, whether she ran up or down hill. The air, the wind, the sea – all of it lifted and carried her. She almost felt as if she were flying. This was not joy, it was bliss.

More writing

Fogelklou's physical vitality in advancing age was matched by her undimmed intellect. During the years that followed she published several collections of essays as well as the finale of her autobiography: *Helgon och häxor*, *Resfärdig*, *Form och strålning* and *Minnesbilder och ärenden*. The essays notably disseminate new ideas and introduce remarkable personalities of the time.

Helgon och häxor is devoted to two psychological types that could be each other's opposite – or complement. Some reviewers were shocked by this combination. The thought that witches could be a perversion of sainthood is not alien to Fogelklou who realised that the same gift and life force could find expression in opposite directions. We all have potential for anything and everything.

The essay on Simone Weil is the first presentation of this remarkable woman to a Swedish audience. Her life and writing have since become much more generally known. Weil has come to be regarded as a modern saint through her self-effacing commitment, illuminated by mysticism and divine experience. She died at the early age of 33. In her words 'living naked and nailed to the tree of life', Fogelklou sees her essence. 'She was not a solution to problems, but a set of questions, not an answer but a plea, not a conclusion but a challenge.'[31] Weil is by no means easy to approach, driven as she was by a scorching responsibility for humanity which she takes on with an enormous personal integrity which includes apparently pointless self-denial. With great empathy Fogelklou manages to present Simone Weil's great paradoxes with clarifying simplicity. She quotes 'Contact with God is the only sacrament'[32] and 'non-violence is only good if it is *effective* – a radiance whose energy substitutes for muscular strength.'[33]

Surely, says Fogelklou, Weil had a lot in common with the bold and wise women who during the middle ages began to be persecuted as witches, largely because the Church wanted to break their power which was regarded as rivalling that of the clergy.

Helgon och häxor can be seen as part of contemporary feminist debate and this book together with *Borttom Birgitta* was hailed by some critics as by far the most intelligent and searching contribution to feminist thinking of the time.

Form och strålning is prefaced by a quote from Fogelklou's preoccupation as a student in her Uppsala days: 'How to probe the integrity and honesty of the whole world of the spirit? Not by measuring opinion, but testing the radiance, would be the way.'

Now she sets to work by probing this radiance as reflected in different forms, situations and people. Worth mentioning is her introduction of Teilhard de Chardin, then hardly known in either Sweden or Britain. She discusses of his *Le phénomène humain* (*The phenomenon of Man*): 'the world is heading towards the "omega point" where love will be all'. *Form och strålning* is a discursive book of meditations. Fogelklou trawls wide seas and gathers material that she combines into a kind of eclectic mosaic of quotes and references. Everywhere one encounters reflections of the 'radiance' where physical, cosmic and spiritual elements converge.

The book was well received. The critics were impressed by the ease with which she handled her abundant material and one eminent scientist commented on her essential understanding of the new discoveries in physics and her intelligent use of scientific metaphor.

In *Minnesbilder och ärenden* the most recent and striking essay in this collection deals with Georges Bataille. When Fogelklou wrote it in 1962, the year of his death, he was quite unknown in Sweden although notorious in his native France. Only lately has this French surrealist found a following. Bataille was a virulent opponent of all rational thinking and all forms of morality. He was a cultural revolutionary, fascinated by the possibility of escaping the human condition by violence and eroticism; the ultimate goal for any intellectual, religious or artistic endeavour should be to destroy the rational individual in a violent transcendental communion. He combined this extreme view with a sharp intellect and was for many years editor of the influential magazine *Critique*.

How could this controversial figure have captured Fogelklou's interest? Did he not push the limits a bit too far? But she had noted Bataille's *L'éxpérience intérieure* (The inner experience) in a survey of recent French literature and been fascinated by his way of experiencing spiritual torments like physical pain. There was much in Bataille she could identify with, e.g. his 'The person who doesn't die from being human will never be human' and 'Spiritual experience *awakens* one'. Also his humility: 'I have no creed to preach. But I have a secret: a surrendering of the self.'[34]

At this time Fogelklou had not yet read his extreme sado-erotic *Ma mère* (My mother) and when she did, her first impulse was to burn the book. But she did not, nor did she give up. She sensed a living soul right through his chaotic way of writing, defended him against the official French condemnation at the time. Her appreciation has been vindicated by later avant-garde critics and Bataille's collected works are now available in ten volumes.

Emilia Fogelklou, now 84, travelled up to the small northern town Härnösand to give a talk on Bataille for a literary society: 'It isn't just Stockholm that needs new ideas.' One wonders what the local townspeople thought!

Resfärdig, the third of Emilia Fogelklou's memoirs covers her life from Arnold's death to the moment of writing. 'Arnold had gone. And no calling came to claim her who was left behind.'[35]

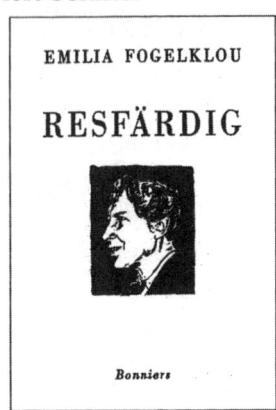

It begins when she was 51, unsure of what direction her life would take, but prepared for anything that could accord with the ethics of their life and her own inner compass. The title suggests departure; Fogelklou was 'ready to go' in more than one sense: ready to set out on journeys, which for her always had a spiritual dimension, but one can also see her life after Arnold as a long preparation for leaving it. There is also an element of closing the accounts of a life that reveals both humility and confidence, a spirit of serving and the certainty of a purpose. She is the prophet, the seer, at the same time as 'the most ordinary person', though in this book Fogelklou does not reach out with any particular message – her purpose is to review her tentative efforts to find a foothold in a life that was so 'scraped bare' without Arnold.

Compared with the poignant and subtle relationships described in *Arnold*, this book largely reflects external activities. Names, destinies, journeys and a variety of tasks crowd the busy life Emilia made hers after Arnold's death. The many details make it a rich document of the time, but the presentation is more fragmented than in the earlier books. Fogelklou also played down the contribution she had made in the early days of many an enterprise, and several of those who were there and had taken part ruefully note that there is little evidence of how inspiring she was at the outset and how supportive in the ongoing work.

The book had a mixed reception. But the eminent E.Hj.Linder was struck by how the Quaker spirit 'on several occasions and because of its freedom from dogmas and Church organisation, has been able to express something extremely valuable about human solidarity on a religious basis; and it has offered comprehensible and useful examples of action.' This critic is one who has understood Emilia Fogelklou's uniqueness of vision: 'Only now have we been presented with a cosmos that fits "the inner world" ... *Only now* we have actually a chance to attain some harmony between faith and science ... Only now.'[36]

Resfärdig ends with a plea for life and to people who create it: 'Why doesn't generous giving blossom amongst people in our world? Couldn't one – both metaphorically and actually – say that we cling to old concepts of reality as essentially consisting of *boundaries*, despite the fact that its nature is *radiation*?'[37]

In this spirit, and in the same year that *Resfärdig* was published, Fogelklou held a series of lectures in Stockholm on 'Seeking in Art, Poetry, Prayer' which formed the core text of *Form och strålning*.

Women were now gradually being admitted to higher posts in society, but the Church was persistent in its resistance to women priests. The synod of 1957 took up this question and Emilia Fogelklou characteristically thought it would be a defeat for the Church more than for the women if the barriers were not removed for women to be ordained.

In the beginning of the 1960s Fogelklou moved to a retirement home in Djursholm, the area where she used to teach fifty years earlier, just outside Stockholm. 'I miss Högfors and the real country, but if only I can walk by the Baltic I'm fine' she writes to a friend.[38] Emilia was over 80, still active and with an alert and unprejudiced mind, interested in current affairs. With undiminished relish for contact with people she was also a very social animal, only hampered by an increasing deafness. She still took part in symposia and lectured. To an onlooker she could look quite feeble and fragile, but as soon as she got onto the podium she was so captivated by her subject that 'her body was crackling with life and her eyes started sending sparks out to her listeners', as one member of her audience put it.

Emilia lecturing. Drawing by Siri Derkert 1966

While she gradually lost most of her old friends, she made plenty of new ones in the younger generation. One of them called her 'a 90-year-old whirlwind'! In the Stockholm underground station of Östermalmstorg there is homage to Emilia Fogelklou and other exceptional women of her era. Images and words inscribed in cement cover the whole length of the two walls opposite the platforms by the artist Siri Derkert.

Ili ageing

> *'Death is in no way frightening, but the magnitude of life and its memories loom so much larger.'* letter 8.12.1965

Emilia Fogelklou never took on the dignity of old age, but liked being on familiar terms, 'Ili' or 'Tili' to most people she knew. Extrovert and active, few people would realise that even at this advanced age Fogelklou was not spared long states of depression. Memories of old disappointments assailed her and she was getting forgetful and very tired. But mostly she rose to the challenge, having an irresistible resilience and faith in what could be achieved with co-operation. One vignette could be cited. During her Djursholm retirement when she was well over eighty, she heard that one of her friends, Margareta Larson, suffered from advanced cancer and had not long to live. Emilia asked her out for a visit to Djursholm, with a promise to meet her at the train. This was in the middle of a freezing winter. Margareta hesitated, but accepted. She found Ili waiting on the platform, but when they set out for her flat, Margareta saw a steep slope rising ahead, covered with ice. 'I'm afraid I can't manage this one!' she says to Ili who replies 'If we hold hands and make a run for it we'll be ok.' And so they did and got up safely. Margareta foiled all doctors' predictions and lived on till 95. In the company of Ili one became more alive oneself.

Infirmity did not hinder her from travelling – for two consecutive years she went down to a Danish folk high school whose principal she had got to know at Woodbrooke some thirty years earlier. Here Fogelklou talked to a group of students about the new archaeological finds in Sumeria and what evidence there was of a matriarchal culture, a subject she was possibly more familiar with than anybody else at this time. Another time she discussed subjects like Martin Buber's *I – Thou* just out in Danish, and the significance of the second Vatican Council Meeting and Pope John XXIII. Emilia Fogelklou remained very interested in what was going on. When the World Council of Churches was held in Uppsala in 1968, a unique event in that the council meets only every seven years at different venues in the world, Emilia Fogelklou attended – naturally, despite her 90 years.

She never lost her intense love of nature: something as simple as a tree in blossom or the play of sunlight in the leaves of the tree outside her window gladdened and refreshed her spirit. Everyone who came to see her was given some parting gift from her bookshelf. So Emilia Fogelklou's considerable library, which also had been Arnold's, was scattered to the winds of all visiting friends. And when the shelves were almost empty they were given a flower or a fruit to take home.

Life was however a school she was longing to leave. The summer of 1972, soon after her 94th birthday she broke her hip in a fall. Well-meaning hospital staff kept her alive through agonising treatment until at last her longing 'to go home' was answered on the 26th September. Emilia and Arnold now rest together in the country churchyard in Skåne next to the vicarage where Arnold grew up. On his stone there is a quotation from the *Divine Comedy*, on hers the words 'There is light yet'.

The whole of the Swedish press, local as well as national papers, strewed roses. She was called 'Sweden's only saint' and 'Sweden's only female genius' – which it was fortunate that she could not read, as she had a horror of praise – especially in print. And yet Fogelklou has several features in common with medieval saints, as some critics observed, above all her passionate religious commitment, which to her was a commitment to life. It had taken her on a path of exploration, which made her a forerunner in many fields, a pioneer with a mystical insight. Her work is of lasting importance; in her spiritual approach to life she is relevant to all times: 'Emilia Fogelklou is a yeast slowly leavening the age, the full effect of which is yet to come', as her friend Margareta Larson put it. The search for a deeper spirituality in the present day goes on, and even as this is written, several scholars and students are researching her work and impact, giving it a fuller attention than it ever had in her lifetime.

Her challenge to us as individuals remains undiminished: Emilia Fogelklou has the last word with a quotation from 'Attempts to understand', the essays from *Medan gräset gror II* that she regarded as central to her work:

'It is not enough that something happens to one; one must also have the strength to really *work through* what has occurred. But life exacts a price, for life is a giver. The more it costs the more it will be worth.'[39]

'There in my God's world all potentials glowed as possibilities. Here on my sentry duty in the actual world I see them stained, bungled and botched by my inability to let God's music play on all the strings of my being, while I at most can make a single life-thread throb, which I can express in action. And in spite of this suffering due to my own limitation, I *must* act, I must let all rich potential be absorbed in some single real creative act. For woe is me if this is not done.'[40]

EMILIA FOGELKLOU
CHRONOLOGY OF LIFE, LETTERS AND SELECT BIBLIOGRAPHY

(All Swedish titles were published in Stockholm)

1878	Born 20 July in Simrishamn, Skåne
1894	Finishes schooling in Kristianstad
1899	Completes Teacher Training in Stockholm. Her first post at Landskrona Secondary School for Girls
1901–05	Teaches at a radical co-educational school in Gothenburg. Studies sociology and philosophy
1902	29 May – has an spiritual inner experience of such power that it will guide her life
1903	*Allvarsstunder* (Quiet Times) *Om religionsundervisningen* (On the teaching of RE)
1906	Fil.kand. (B.A.) is completed in one year. The five subjects: history of religion, theoretical and practical philosophy, history of literature and pedagogy
1907	*Frans av Assisi* (St Francis of Assisi), reprinted 1922, 1972, 1981
1909	First woman to achieve a Bachelor of Divinity in Sweden
1910–11	Olaus Petri scholarship. Travels in Europe for the purpose of studying 'current philosophical and religious movements'
1911	*Medan gräset gror* I&II (While the grass grows I&II)
1911–15	Teaches at Djursholm's Co-educational School
1913	*Allvarsstunder* II (Quiet Times II). Study trip to Iceland
1914	Arnold Norlind sends her his first Dante Canto in translation for Christmas
1915	EF's father dies. EF travels to the Hague as one of the Swedish delegates to the Women's Peace Conference
1915–16	Takes a sabbatical year in order to write
1915	*Förkunnare* (Preachers)
1916	*Från hövdingen till den törnekrönte* (1916 *From Chieftain to the Crown of Thorns*) *Från längtansvägarna* (1916 *From the Paths of Longing*) *Ur fromhetslivets svensk-historia* I&II (1916, 1917 *The History of Spiritual Life in Sweden*)

CHRONOLOGY 187

1916–18 Teacher and co-worker at Birkagården

1917 Co-editor and translator of *Legender från Sveriges medeltid* (Legends from the Swedish Middle Ages)

1918–23 Senior lecturer at the Teacher's Training College, Kalmar

1919 *Birgitta* (1955, 1973)
Protestant och katolik (1937, Protestant and Catholic)

1920 Sick-leave because of severe eye condition
Från själens vägar (From the Paths of the Spirit)

1920–21 Cares for her sick mother and sister until their end

1921 Journey to London. Then continues to Berlin to meet Arnold

1922 Marries Arnold Norlind. They settle in Lillstugan, a small cottage in Jakobsberg, near Stockholm

1923–28 Lectures in ethics and psychology at the Institute for Social Studies, Stockholm

1923 'Drömtydaren' ('The Dream Interpreter'), *Barnbiblioteket Saga*:95

1924 *Vila och arbete* (Leisure and Work)

1925 *Befriaren* (The Liberator)

1926 *Samhällstyper och medborgarideal* (Social Types and Social Ideals)
Människan och hennes arbete (People and Work)

1927 *Skolliv och själsliv* (School Life and Spiritual Life)

1929 *Kväkaren James Nayler* (1931 James Nayler, The Rebel Saint)
Arnold dies 17th February
Samarbetets psykologi och förvärvslivet (The Psychology of Co-operation and Gainful Employment)

1929–30 Travels to the USA on a grant to study sociology and applied psychology at Columbia University

1931 *Den allra vanligaste människan* (The Most Ordinary Human Being)
Om psykisk hälsovård (On Mental Health Care)
'Luther and Fox', a paper presented at the Amsterdam International Conference of Friends

1933–4 Fellowship of Woodbrooke College, Birmingham

1934–5 Seriously ill

1935 *William Penn*. Convalescent at Fogelstad during the spring. In co-operation with others starts the Swedish branch of the Religious Society of Friends

1937 *Psykologiska faktorer i samband med krig och fred* (Psychological Factors in Relation to the Question of War and Peace)

1938	Applies for a chair in the History of Religion with the Psychology of Religion at Uppsala University, but is declared incompetent during spring 1939
1939	Lectures at the Quaker college Pendle Hill, USA in the summer. In the autumn undertakes relief-work for Jews in Berlin
1940	Visits Finland during the war. Studies and works at the Institute for Medical Psychology and Psychotherapy in Stockholm
1941	Sweden's first woman Honorary Doctor of Divinity *Bortom Birgitta* (Beyond Birgitta) Relief work. Central figure in the formation of IAL, Internationella arbetslag (International Work-camps)
1944	*Arnold*
1944–5	Journey to Britain to study rebuilding work
1946	Move to her friend Florrie Hamilton's manor house Högfors, north of Stockholm *Ljus finns ändå* (There is Light Still)
1946–8	Runs a counselling service at Västerås
1947	Journeys to Finland and Germany for rebuilding work
1950	*Barhuvad* (Bareheaded)
1951	Settles for a while in Lund, but returns to Högfors Travels to Israel and Greece
1952	*Helgon och häxor* (Saints and Witches)
1954	*Resfärdig* (Ready to Go)
1958	*Form och strålning* (Form and Radiance)
1962	Moves to a retirement home in Djursholm
1963	*Minnesbilder och ärenden* (Memories and messages)
1966	Moves to a retirement home in Uppsala
1972	Dies in Uppsala 26 September

TWO POSTHUMOUS COLLECTIONS OF LETTERS

1979	*Brev till vännerna* (Letters to My Friends)
1988	*Kära Ili, käraste Elin* (Dear Ili, dearest Elin)

SELECTION IN ENGLISH

1985	*Reality and Radiance: Selected Autobiographical Works of Emilia Fogelklou* trans. H.T. Lutz (Richmond, Indiana)

GLOSSARY OF PEOPLE, PLACES AND EVENTS

Alexander, Horace 1889–1989, British Quaker, internationally active. Personal friend to Gandhi and mediator in India's struggle for independence from British rule.

Antigone mythological figure, heroine in Sophocles' drama, who has become the emblem of personal integrity in the face of tyranny.

Bachofen, Johann 1815–87, Swiss lawyer. Through his work *Das Mutterrecht* he was one of the pioneers of comparative legal science.

Barnett, Samuel Augustus 1844–1913, English clergyman and social reformer; ardent philanthropist and first warden of Toynbee Hall. B. wrote the highly influential *Practicable Socialism* together with his wife Henrietta Octavia Rowland.

Bataille, Georges 1897–1962, French author and philosopher; librarian.

Beckius, Greta 1886–1912, took her degree at Uppsala 1909. Wrote a novel about the plight of women students in a world of men, *Marit Grene*, 1911. Subsequently she took her life.

Bendixson, Artur b. 1859, organiser and head of the progressive Gothenburg High School from its start in 1901 until 1904.

Bergman, Hugo 1883–1975, university lecturer, became the first rector of the new Hebrew University of Jerusalem.

Bergson, Henri 1859–1941, of Irish extraction, naturalised French, one of the most influential philosophers of his time. B. defines reality as duration and movement in contrast to earlier philosophies. Intuition is the highest form of consciousness. Nobel prize for lit. in 1927.

Beskow, Natanael 1865–1953, preacher, educator and author. B. had studied theology and art, but left both to become headmaster of the progressive co-educational Djursholm High School and an independent preacher at Djursholm chapel 1896–1931. B. had strong social and pacifist leanings. Head of Birkagården until 1946.

Birgitta (Saint) 1303–1373, Sweden's only saint, daughter of one the most powerful men in the land. B. lived ascetically, caring for the sick and the poor. She experienced visions from an early age. Her nine books of Revelations are remarkable medieval documents.

Birkagården created by Natanael Beskow and Ebba Pauli in 1912, as a 'settlement' to relieve the plight of the poor.

Bjerre, Poul 1876–1964, Swedish physician, author, psychotherapist and psychoanalyst. Initially greatly influenced by Freud; later B. developed his own system he called 'psychosynthesis'.

Björck, Staffan 1915–1995, Swedish professor, literature historian, critic.

Blake, William 1757–1827, English mystic, poet and artist of considerable visionary power.

Bobrikov, Nikolaj Russian General governor of Finland who attempted a complete russification of Finland 1898–1904, until a student's bullet ended his life.

Borelius, Hilma 1869–1932, daughter of Jacob B. First woman to be a senior lecturer in the history of lit. at Univ. of Lund in 1910. Also very involved in the feminist movement.

Borelius, Jacob 1823–1909, Swedish philosopher.

Boström, Christopher Jacob 1797–1866, Swedish philosopher; instigator of the only original philosophical system in 19th C. Sweden, according to which ultimate reality is God. Every human being corresponds to an eternal idea. B. was fairly radical in his philosophy: he denied the divinity of Christ and the teaching of Hell. B.'s rational idealism had many followers.

Braque, Georges 1882–1963, French artist working for a period in close collaboration with Picasso.

Bremer, Fredrika 1801–65, author, social reformer. Pioneer of the Swedish feminist movement.

Brinton, Howard 1884–1973, U.S. Quaker who together with his wife Anna was Head of Studies at the U.S. Quaker College, Pendle Hill 1936–54. Author of several religious books; delegate to the third Quaker World Conference in 1952.

Brinton, Anna wife of Howard B.

Buber, Martin 1878–1965, Jewish philosopher of religion, from 1938 Prof. of Social Philosophy at Jerusalem. As a philosopher B. is mostly known for his principle of dialogue, *I and Thou* (1923).

Cadbury, George 1839–1922, British manufacturer and philanthropist. Created the garden village of Bourneville, near Birmingham, for his employees. It became a model of its kind. Initiated and financed Woodbrooke Quaker College.

Carson, Rachel 1907–64, American marine biologist and author. Her widely read *Silent Spring*, 1962, introduced the environmental debate on the use of chemical pesticides.

Catherine of Siena (Saint) c.1347–80, it was largely owing to her efforts that the Pope moved back to Rome from Avignon. C. is together with St. Francis the patron saint of Italy.

Chagall, Marc 1887–1985, Russian painter working mainly in Paris.

Chardin, Jean-Baptiste 1699–1779, French painter who created little masterpieces of atmospheric interiors and still lives with a shimmering play of colour of unsurpassed lustre.

Cromwell, Oliver 1599–1658, English soldier and statesman. A strict puritan and an excellent commander, leader of the so called 'Ironsides', a regiment in the army of Parliament against the King's.

Dante Alighieri 1265–1321, Florentine poet, wrote his *Divina Commedia* 1313–21 (*The Divine Comedy*).

Darwin, Charles 1809–82, British biologist who together with Alfred Wallace presented the revolutionary theory of evolution, as set out in D.'s *On the Origin of Species by means of Natural Selection* (1859).

Derkert, Siri 1888–1973, Swedish artist who began in the fauve and cubist tradition, but later developed her own style of great simplification. Socially aware, she was drawn to the spirited struggle of many individuals and has made a whole series of portraits of the Fogelstad women.

Dewey, John 1859–1952, U.S. philosopher and pedagogue. D. has been called 'the father of modern education': the activity and interest of the child should be the basis of teaching methods.

Djursholm 'garden city' suburb just north of Stockholm.

Djursholm Chapel created by private subscription, consecrated in 1902.

Djursholm High School a private institution in EF's time.

Eckhart, Johannes, 'Meister Eckhart' c.1260–1327, German philosopher, the first of the great Western speculative mystics. According to E. the Divine element permeates all living things, but is especially manifest in the human soul, whose purpose is to find union with God.

Engels, Friedrich 1820–95, German radical socialist.

Feuerbach, Ludwig 1804–72, German philosopher who abandoned his early idealism for a materialist view in his main work *Das Wesen des Christentums*, 1841 (1854, *The essence of Christianity*). F.'s criticism of Christianity greatly influenced the younger generation working for social reform, esp. Marx and Engels. F.'s expression 'Der Mensch ist was er isst' ('Man is what he eats'), comes from a review of 1850.

Fogelklou, Birger (Bie) older brother to EF

Fogelklou, Ernst eldest brother

Fogelklou, Gertrud (Gert) younger sister

Fogelklou, Johan father

Fogelklou, Johanna (Nan) twin sister

Fogelklou, Josefina (Fej) twin sister, married to Johannes Liedholm

Fogelklou, Maria mother

Fogelstad country estate owned by Lisse Tamm who used it to create the first college for women workers.

Ford, Henry, 'King of the car' 1863–1947, US industrialist and philanthropist. F.'s initiative in sending his peace ship 'Oscar II' in Dec. 1915 'to get the boys out of the trenches by Christmas' was generally regarded as creditable to his heart if not his head.

Fox, George 1624–91, the religious leader of the Quakers. G.F.'s *Journal*, publ. 1694, is a document of great historical and autobiographical value.

Fox, Marion 1861–1949, British Quaker. One of the first Friends to visit Germany after 1919 for relief work. Also became a close friend of EF with whom she kept a lively correspondence. A selection of their letters is included in *Marion Fox, Quaker*, ed. H.Fox, London, 1951.

Fra Angelico c.1387–1455, Italian Dominican monk and artist. As a monk he was given the name *Fra Giovanni di Fiesole*. In 1436 he was called to Florence by the Medicis to paint the frescos in the St Marco monastery. In his unified treatment of perspective, colour and light we find piety expressed in its most clear and pure form.

Francis of Assisi (Saint) c.1181–1226. Canonised 1228.

Freud, Sigmund 1856–1939, Austrian physician. Founded psychoanalysis, after applying the method to himself: *Die Traumdeutung* (1900, *The Interpretation of Dreams*)

Gandhi, Mohandras Karamchand; 'Mahatma' (Great Spirit) 1869–1948, Indian politician. Studied law in London; developed a method of passive resistance, a refusal to obey which according to G. is a more effective weapon than armed resistance. Led the Indian liberation from British rule in India.

George, Henry 1839–97, U.S. journalist and economist; self taught, who had started as sailor and gold digger. His work *Progress and Poverty* (1879) was translated into many languages. He recommended the nationalisation of land and that all taxes should be replaced by a land tax.

Giotto di Bondone c.1266–1337, Italian artist, famous for his frescos in Assisi, Padua and Florence. Influenced by St Francis, G. tried to make Biblical reality accessible to everyone.

Hägerström, Axel 1868–1939, Swedish philosopher who totally rejected ideal metaphysics. H. had a great following and founded the influential

GLOSSARY OF PEOPLE, PLACES AND EVENTS 193

'Uppsala School' of philosophy.

Hague Women's Peace Conference April 28–May 1st 1915, chaired by Jane Addams.

Hamilton, Florrie of a Swedish noble family. She owned the iron works and manor house at Högfors where she extended considerable hospitality.

Harnack, Adolf von 1851–1930, German theologian. Figurehead of liberal theology at the end of 19TH C. *Das Wesen des Christentums*, 1900 (1901, *What is Religion*) expresses H.'s vision of a Christianity free from dogma.

Harvey, Edmund 1875–1955, British civil servant, M.P. and writer. Philanthropist and Warden of Toynbee Hall 1904–11. Quaker.

Hesselblad, Sr Elisabeth 1870–1957, follower of St Birgitta and founder of a new Birgittine convent.

Hitler, Adolf 1889–1945

Högfors 1. Small town, formerly mining community.
2. Manor house and iron works owned by Florrie Hamilton in the Bergslagen mining area northwest of Stockholm.

Hügel, Friedrich von 1852–1925, British Catholic lay theologian of Austrian descent, one of the main figures in the Catholic Modernist Movement. In his work *The Mystical Element of Religion* he stresses the mystical element in all religions.

Huxley, Aldous 1894–1963, British author. His most widely read work is *Brave New World*, 1932, a satire on the totalitarian state.

Ibsen, Henrik 1828–1906, Norwegian dramatist

Isherwood, Christopher 1904–86, British-American writer. Author of *Goodbye to Berlin*, 1939, a description of Berlin in the 1930s, from which the musical *Cabaret* was made in 1966.

Jacobs, Aletta 1854–1929, first woman physician in Holland. Pacifist.

Jacobsson, Malte 1885–1966, county governor

Jakobsberg suburb of Stockholm

James, William 1842–1910, U.S. philosopher and psychologist. Brother of the writer Henry James. Like Bergson W.J. stressed the importance of intuition and creativity rather than logic. His work has inspired world wide research in the psychology of religion.

Johanson, Klara (KJ) 1875–1948, Swedish writer, journalist and eminent critic of literature.

Jones, Rufus 1863–1948, U.S. professor of philosophy at Haverford university for 30 years. Over 50 published works. Visited Germany in 1938 with two other Quakers to arrange with Gestapo leaders for emigration of

Jews from Nazi-held territories. Quaker.

Kalmar on the Baltic coast, boasting the magnificent renaissance Kalmar castle and facing the island of Öland.

Keijser, Gustaf 1844–1916, Swedish lecturer in Religious Studies. Formed the Boström Society in 1908, for the dissemination of studies on the philosopher Boström.

Kellgren, Johan Henrik 1751–1795, Swedish writer and critic.

Key, Ellen 1849–1926, Swedish author, educator and feminist. Popular lecturer at Workers' Societies. After achieving international fame by 1900, she devoted all her time to writing, travel and lecturing.

Kierkegaard, Søren 1813–55, Danish writer and philosopher. His stress on the responsibility of the individual has caused him to be counted as the father of existentialism. His work has greatly influenced other writers and theologians by its intellectual clarity and intensity.

Kivik small fishing port and market town on the Baltic coast near Simrishamn.

Kollwitz, Käthe 1867–1945, German graphic artist, movingly depicting the poor in society.

Kreuger, Ivar 1880–1932, Swedish financier who built an industrial empire. Its collapse, in the wake of the Wall Street crash reverberated round the world.

Kristianstad Swedish garrison town in the province of Skåne, founded by the Danish king Kristian IV in 1622 as a fortification against the Swedes.

Lagerlöf, Selma 1858–1940, novelist; the first Swedish woman author to receive the Nobel Prize for Literature in 1909.

Landquist, John 1881–1974, Swedish philosopher.

Landskrona town on the south coast of Skåne, southern Sweden.

Larson, Margareta 1905–2000, teacher, devoted friend of EF.

Larsson, Hans 1862–1944, Swedish philosopher, known for his writing on intuition and *The Logic of Poetry* 1899, where he claims that intuitive synthesis requires strict logic and the unified effort of human faculties. L. regards emotion as an important factor in consciousness.

Levander, Hans born 1914, Swedish critic, author and lexicographer.

Liedholm, Johannes husband to Fej, EF's sister

Liedholm, Rickard (Titten) their son, EF's godson.

Lillstugan Arnold's and Emilia's cottage in Jakobsberg.

Linder, Erik Hjalmar 1906–1994, Swedish author and critic, professor of Swedish lit.

GLOSSARY OF PEOPLE, PLACES AND EVENTS 195

Linderholm, Emanuel 1872–1937, professor and theologian.

Lindqvist, Sven Born 1932, Swedish author.

Lund Ancient university city on the Skåne coast in southern Sweden.

Lutz, Howard 1921–91, U.S. professor of history at the University of Wisconsin, Eau Claire. Lived and worked for some years in Scandinavia. Quaker.

Luther, Martin 1483–1546, German monk and theologian, leader of the Reformation in Germany. L. formed the League of Protestantism which in its stress on the faith of the individual and religious liberty stood in opposition to Roman Catholicism.

Lönborg, Sven 1871–1959, Swedish historian and geographer; teacher, headmaster and reformer. Writer on religious education, historical topics and Classical Antiquity.

Macmurray, John 1891–1976, British philosopher, professor of philosophy at University College London and of Moral Philosophy at the University of Edinburgh. Quaker.

Malthus, Thomas 1766–1834, English economist. His *An Essay on the Principle of Population* was published anonymously in 1798, arousing a storm of controversy, subsequently with six revised editions. Influenced Darwin.

Mann, Thomas 1875–1955, German novelist. Awarded the Nobel prize for literature in 1929.

Marx, Karl 1818–83, German social scientist and revolutionary.

Maynard, Mary A.B. (Mab) 1864–1944, British teacher and Settlement worker. For 14 years a member of Friends Service Council, serving on the Scandinavia and Germany Committees; friend and translator of Fredrika Bremer. Quaker.

Michelsen, Ellen 1885–1959, Swedish teacher and author. Friend of EF.

Moore, George 1873–1958, British, very influential prof. of Moral Philosophy, leading the Cambridge School of Philosophy and one of the founders of modern analytical philosophy.

Murray, Margaret 1863–1963, British Egyptologist at University College London. She also published the highly controversial *The witch-cult in Western Europe* in 1921.

Mussolini, Benito 1883–1945. Leader of the Italian fascist party 1920–45.

Napoleon I 1769–1821 has at times been hero-worshipped by the young.

Nayler, James 1618–60, one of the pioneers of the Quaker movement.

Nerman, Ture 1886–1969, Swedish author and radical journalist.

Nietzsche, Friedrich 1844–1900, German philosopher and poet. As a student influenced by Schopenhauer, but later rejected his pessimism.

N. is mostly known for his affirmation of the Superman.

Norberg Mining village in Bergslagen, north of Stockholm.

Norlind, Arnold 1883–1929, husband of EF

Öland long narrow chalky island in the Baltic, renowned for its unique varieties of flora and fauna.

Olaus Petri 1493–1552, Swedish priest, profound humanist and chief architect of the Reformation in Sweden.

Olaus Petri Society founded in honour of the above to promote international religious and philosophical studies.

Oljelund, Ivan 1892–1978, Swedish journalist and political activist. Imprisoned for over a year for his pacifist action in time of war.

Parker, Emily American Quaker who worked with American Friends Service Committee in Spain 1938–39.

Pauli, Ebba 1873–1941, Swedish educator; an energetic and efficient worker in a number of social institutions. She was co-principal with N. Beskow of Birkagården 1912–36.

Pendle Hill Quaker college, centre for study and contemplation in Wallingford, Pennsylvania.

Penn, William 1644–1718, English Quaker, founder of Pennsylvania as a colony, for which he wrote a constitution in 1683.

Pestalozzi, Johann Heinrich 1746–1827, Swiss educational reformer whose ideas and practices had a far-reaching effect on educational methods.

Pius X 1835–1914, pope from 1903 who, despite his reactionary attitude to the modernist movement, carried out several liturgical and ecclesiastical reforms.

Picasso, Pablo 1881–1973, Spanish painter working in Paris.

Puvis de Chavannes, Pierre Cécile 1824–98, French artist. P. was highly successful in his lifetime, acquiring the reputation as the foremost mural painter of his generation.

Rilke, Rainer Maria 1875–1926, Austrian lyric poet. After his studies he made several journeys, e.g. to Italy and Russia, where he was influenced by Tolstoy and Russian Orthodox Christianity. In Sweden he came into close contact with Ellen Key. Was secretary for a time to Rodin, which resulted in *Auguste Rodin* (1913). Later followed the famous *Duino Elegies* (1923) and the *Sonnets to Orpheus* (1923)

Rodin, Auguste 1840–1917, highly successful French sculptor. R.'s work combines a remarkable realism with great expressiveness, often with a symbolic dimension. *The Thinker* was created in 1880.

Ruskin John 1819–1900, British writer on art and social reform. Champion

GLOSSARY OF PEOPLE, PLACES AND EVENTS

of Turner in *Modern Painters*, of which the first of five volumes appeared in 1843.

Russell, Bertrand 1872–1970, British philosopher.

Schwimmer, Rosika 1877–1948, Hungarian musician, peaceworker.

Simrishamn EF's native town on the east coast of Skåne.

Skåne Sweden's southernmost province.

Socrates 469–399 BC great Greek philosopher who made enemies by showing up those who had a reputation for wisdom by his superior argument. He was sentenced to death by drinking hemlock and made a speech before taking the poison.

Söderberg, Boel Swedish teacher and writer on education.

Söderblom, Nathan 1866–1931, Swedish theologian; archbishop. Internationally leading figure of the ecumenical movement.

Sorbonne older name for the University of Paris.

Spinoza, Baruch 1632–77, Jewish philosopher of Portuguese origin, who rejected the Cartesian dualism of spirit and matter and saw only 'one infinite substance'.

Steere, Douglas V 1901–1995, US. Professor of Philosophy at Harverford College. Travelled widely in Europe on pastoral visits to Quaker groups and for his own research. Closely associated with Friedrich von Hügel. Quaker.

Stein, Gertrude 1874–1946, American writer, living in Paris from 1902.

Stolpe, Sven 1905–96, Swedish author and critic.

Strindberg, August 1849–1912, Swedish dramatist and novelist

Sundberg, Per 1889–1947, Swedish educator and peace activist. Founded the residential Viggbyholm School 1928 for children with special needs. Several peace conferences were held there during vacations. Quaker.

Tagore, Rabindranath 1861–1941, prolific Indian writer whose poetry and prose are imbued with a sense of the beauty of the universe, a love of simplicity and sense of the divine, expressing the spirit of the Bengali people.

Tamm, Elisabeth (Lisse) 1880–1958, Swedish landowner, socially and politically active, one of the first women MPs.

T'ang Dynasty of Chinese emperors that ruled China for nearly 300 years, AD 618–907.

Teilhard de Chardin, Pierre 1881–1955, French Jesuit priest, philosopher, mystic and geologist. Columbia University, Manhattan, New York City.

Thoreau, Henry 1817–62, American author, studied at Harvard, profoundly influenced by Emerson.

Thorvall, Dagny (Tove) 1883–1933, Swedish teacher and co-worker at Birkagården where she initiated a meditation circle out of which Sweden's first group of Quakers was formed.

Uppsala cathedral city of medieval origin north of Stockholm.

Uppsala University Sweden's first university, founded in 1477.

Vanås Manor in Skåne, famous for its collection of paintings.

Västerås town in central Sweden

Wahlström, Lydia 1869–1954, Swedish historian, educator, author.

Weininger, Otto 1880–1903, Austrian philosopher.

Whitman, Walt 1819–1892, American poet. *Leaves of Grass* first published 1855, an unconventional free verse celebration of individual freedom and brotherhood with strong sexual connotations.

Wicksteed, Philip, 1844–1927, British Unitarian preacher; economist with literary interests: wrote a number of books on Dante, whom he also translated.

Wilde, Oscar 1854–1900, Irish, brilliant author of very successful comedies where the dialogue scintillates with aphoristic wit and spirit.

Wilder, Thornton 1897–1975, American very successful dramatist and novelist. Three of his novels have won the Pulitzer prize.

Woodbrooke Quaker college near Birmingham.

Woolman, John 1720–72, American Quaker preacher, 'a Quaker saint' to many. Anti-slavery campaigner and worked for a more humane treatment of the Indians. His *Journal* was printed in 1774.

World Council of Churches took place in Uppsala in 1968.

Wägner, Elin 1882–1949, Swedish author and journalist. Quaker.

Yapp, Lajla 1887–1941, Swedish historian and translator.

NOTES

I EARLY YEARS

1. *Form och strålning* (Form and Radiance) p 11
2. Dante's *Inferno* (V, 121–123)
3. *Barhuvad* (Bareheaded) p 20
4. *Form och strålning* p 98
5. *Barhuvad* pp.16–17
6. *Form och strålning* p 24
7. *Barhuvad* p 21
8. *Barhuvad* p 35
9. *Medan gräset gror I* (While the grass grows I) p 11
10. 'Om snillet' (On genius) by Johan Henrik Kellgren
11. letter (18.5.1924)
12. Feuerbach *Das Wesen des Christentums* (What is Christianity) 1841
13. *Form och strålning* p 97
14. 'Några opolitiska på kristendomsundervisningens närvarande läge' (Some unpolitical views on the present position of Religious Education) *Arbetssättet i folkskolan VI* (Method in the elementary school) VI, 1928, p 7
15. *Barhuvad* p 35
16. *Form och strålning* p 28
17. *Barhuvad* p 39
18. *Form och strålning* p 163
19. Henry George *Progress and Poverty* (1879)
20. *Barhuvad* p 42
21. *Minnesbilder och ärenden* (Memories and messages) p 51
22. *Barnets århundrade* (The Century of the Child), 1900
23. *Minnesbilder och ärenden* p 46
24. *Barhuvad* p 48
25. *Die Zukunft* (The Future) Jan 1905
26. *Barhuvad* p 50

II REVELATION

1. *Minnesbilder och ärenden* p 51
2. *Barhuvad* p 53
3. letters 3–6.7.1921
4. letter 8.1.1930
5. diary, Italy 28.3.1911
6. *Allvarsstunder* p 96
7. *Allvarsstunder* p 120
8. *Skolan*, nr. 9, 1904, p 22
9. *Skolan* p 20
10. *Skolan* p 15
11. *Barhuvad* p 58
12. *Medan gräset gror I* p 93
13. *Sex and Character*, 1903
14. *Barhuvad* p 64
15. *Times Literary Supplement* 16.2.1906
16. Weininger 'A Conversation about Male and Female' dated 1905 (included in *Medan gräset gror II*)
17. *Medan gräset gror II* p 51
18. *Medan gräset gror II* p 91

19 diary 29.1.1906
20 diary 1.2.1906
21 *Barhuvad* p 67
22 *Barhuvad* p 68
23 *Barhuvad* p 69
24 *Barhuvad* p 76
25 diary 7.5.1906
26 diary. 18.11.1908
27 letter 7.10.1906
28 diary 6.11.1906
29 diary 12.2.1907
30 Ture Nerman, *Olympen, ett gammalt Uppsalahus* (Olympia, an Old House in Uppsala) 1913, p 159
31 diary 29.3.1908
32 *Barhuvad* p 89
33 *Life of St Francis*, Paris, 1895
34 *Frans av Assisi* p 7
35 *Frans av Assisi* p 80
36 diary 3.12.1907
37 diary 3.12.1907
38 diary 18.5.1908
39 diary 6.4.1908
40 *Barhuvad* p 93
41 *Barhuvad* p 103
42 diary 4.1.1909
43 diary 4.1.1909

III CHALLENGES

1 letter 19.3.1910
2 *Vår Lösen*, 1910, p 14–15
3 letter, 21.8.1910
4 *Protestant och katolik*, (*Protestant and Catholic*) 1937, p 61

5 diary 18.10.1910
6 diary 24.10.1910
7 diary 18.10.1910
8 letter 3.8.1920
9 *Barhuvad* p 146
10 *Encycl. Britannia*, 1954, Vol 3, p 435
11 letter 10.7.1912
12 *Från längtansvägarna* (From the paths of longing) p 81
13 *Från längtansvägarna* p 82
14 diary 12.3.1911, referring to a famous incident when Martin Luther is said to have thrown a bottle of ink at the devil in his battles with him.
15 *Barhuvad* p 160
16 diary 26.3.1911
17 diary 16.5.1906
18 diary 28.3.1911
19 diary 28.3.1911
20 letter 31.3.1911
21 *Barhuvad* p 168
22 *Barhuvad* p 168
23 *Barhuvad* p 69
24 Hans Larsson, *Ord & Bild* 1935, p 407
25 *Medan gräset gror II* p 69
26 *Medan gräset gror II* p 22
27 letter p 70
28 letter 11.8.1913
29 letter 23.7.1912
30 *Barhuvad* p 190

IV A WRECKED WORLD

1 letter 22.9.1914

NOTES FOR PAGES 75-112 201

2 letter from Arnold Norlind to Emilia 22.12.1914
3 H. Larsson, *Hemmabyarna* (Local villages) 1916, p 305
4 *Den allra vanligaste människan* p 12
5 diary 26–27.2.1915
6 letter 21.12.1915
7 *Arnold* p 17
8 *Barhuvad* p 200
9 *Barhuvad* p 200
10 letter 3.3.1915
11 *Svenska Dagbladet* 27.7.1952
12 letter 26.12.1917
13 *Från själens vägar* p 71
14 *Från själens vägar* p 63
15 *Från själens vägar* p 71
16 *Barhuvad* p 218
17 *Barhuvad* p 219
18 Quoted by N.Beskow in *Dagny Thorvall in memoriam*, 1933, p 9
19 letter 17.9.1916
20 *Barhuvad* p 223
21 *Barhuvad* p 228
22 letter 23.10.1916
23 diary 11.6.1917
24 letter 26.12.1917
25 *Barhuvad* p 231
26 *Barhuvad* p 232
27 *Barhuvad* p 237
28 letter 23.7.1918
29 *Klarnad syn* (Cleared Vision) 1935
30 *Minnesbilder och ärenden* p 65
31 letter 25.10.1918
32 *Barhuvad* p 242
33 letter 23.11.1919
34 *Barhuvad* p 239
35 letter 18.4.1919
36 *Barhuvad* p 244
37 letter 9.2.1919
38 letter 10.4.1919
39 *Barhuvad* p 244
40 letter 30.3.1921
41 *Birgitta* p 88
42 *Birgitta* p 145
43 *Birgitta* p 186
44 S.Stolpe's postscript to *Birgitta* (1973 ed.) p 224
45 *Ord & Bild*, 1935, p 411
46 *Det andliga nutidsläget och kyrkan II* (The Present Spiritual Situation and the Church) 1919, p 116
47 letter 17.10.1919
48 letter 26.5.1919
49 *Barhuvad* p 253
50 *Barhuvad* p 255
51 *Från själens vägar* p 173
52 *Från själens vägar* p 173
53 *Från själens vägar* p 194
54 *Ord & Bild*, 1935, p 411
55 letter 21.12.1920
56 letter 30.3.1921
57 letter 1.7.1921

V ARNOLD & EMILIA

1 *Arnold* p 33
2 Malte Jacobsson, *Minnesbilder*, (Remembered Images) 1964, p 51

NOTES FOR PAGES 114-147

3 Arnold's diary 2.9.1913
4 *Arnold* p 112
5 *Arnold* p.49–51
6 letter 1.11.1921
7 letter 1.11.1921
8 letter p 58
9 letter p 185
10 letter to Emilia 24.1.1922
11 letter to Emilia 7.5.1922
12 letter 3.3.1921
13 letter 18.6.1917
14 *Arnold* p 223
15 *Arnold* p 232
16 letter 8.81929
17 letter 21.8.1910
18 letter 17.3.1917
19 letter 18.5.1924
20 letter 8.1.1925
21 *Arnold* p 239
22 letter 17.9.1916
23 *Det andliga nutidsläget och kyrkan II* (The Present Spiritual Situation and the Church) 1919, p 119
24 *Skola och samhälle* p 119
25 *Skola och samhälle* p 237
26 Boel Söderberg, *I döda pedagogers sällskap*, (Dead Pedagogues' Society) 1995
27 letter 18.5.1924
28 letter 6.6.1924
29 diary 1.2.1952
30 Quoted at the Memorial Service 10.10.1972
31 letter 19.1.1924
32 letter 7.3.1917

33 K. Johanson in letter to Emilia 26.5.1919
34 *Järfälla hembygdsblad*, 1987:4
35 letter 16.2.1924
36 letter 18.5.1924
37 letter 9.11.1926
38 *Hertha*, 1915 p 298
39 letter 11.10.1930
40 *Dagens Nyheter*, 27.9.1972
41 diary 14.10.1924
42 *Vila och arbete* 1924, *Samhällstyper och medborgarideal* 1926, *Människan och hennes arbete* 1926, *Skolliv och själsliv* 1927, *Samarbetets psykologi och förvärvslivet* 1929.
43 *Vila och arbete* p 19
44 letter 2.8.1925
45 'Kunskapsundervisning eller bekännelseundervisning?' (Teaching Information or Teaching Affirmation?) *Skola och samhälle*, 1926, p 33
46 *Arnold* p 295
47 *Arnold* p 296
48 *Kväkaren James Nayler* p 5
49 For the full text see James Nayler, *Works* (1716) p 696 or Fogelklou, *James Nayler, the Rebel Saint* p 282
50 *James Nayler, the Rebel Saint*, 1931, translated by Lajla Yapp

VI FORSAKEN

1 letter 20.6.1929
2 letter 6.10.1929
3 letter 28.9.1930
4 letter 11.10.1930

5 letter 7.10.1930
6 letter 21.7.1942
7 *Resfärdig* p 33
8 letter dated 'Easter 1931'
9 letter 16.2.1924
10 letter 22.1.1931
11 letter 30.5.1934
12 letter 16.5.1933
13 letter 13.2.1934
14 letter 6.12.1921
15 *Göteborgs-Posten* 5.3.1979
16 letter 10.6.1929
17 *Resfärdig* p 96
18 Margareta Larson, *De arbetade för fred* (They Worked for Peace) 1950, p 208
19 E.Hj.Linder in *Göteborgs-Posten* 5.3.1979
20 *Resfärdig* p 96
21 letter 11.8.1913
22 *Barhuvad* p 103

VII RENEWED ENDEAVOUR

1 letter 23.4.1940
2 letter 2.6.1940
3 letter 19.10.1919; Klara Johanson *Brev* p 108
4 letter 2.6.1940
5 letter 31.12.1940
6 *Afton Tidningen* 1942
7 letter 30.3.1942
8 letter 8.3.1943
9 *Helga* 16.10.1972
10 letter 24.8.1979
11 *Arnold* p 265
12 letter 29.11.1930

13 Sven Lindqvist, *En älskares dagbok* (1981, The Diary of a Lover) p 258
14 *Resfärdig* p 202
15 letter 30.7.1946
16 letter 27.7.1946
17 letter 13.12.1946
18 *Resfärdig* p 234
19 *Resfärdig* p 230
20 *Svenska Dagbladet* 14.10.1923
21 *Resfärdig* p 231
22 Howard Lutz, *Reality and Radiance*, p 12
23 *Ljus finns ändå* p 155
24 *Ljus finns ändå* p 158
25 D.V. Steere's foreword to Lutz, *Reality and Radiance* p 12
26 letter 20.7.1948
27 letter 27.8.1948
28 'Drömtydaren', p 37
29 E.Hj.Linder, *Resor i rum och tid* (Travels in Space and Time) 1956, p 125
30 *Resfärdig*, p 271
31 *Helgon och häxor* p 133
32 *Helgon och häxor* p 131
33 *Helgon och häxor* p 116
34 *Minnesbilder och ärenden*, p 116
35 *Resfärdig* p 5
36 E.Hj.Linder, 1956, p 135
37 *Resfärdig* p 289
38 letter 13.6.1963
39 *Medan gräset gror II* p 55
40 *Medan gräset gror II* p 72

INDEX

Alexander, Horace 174
Allvarsstunder (Quiet Times) 28, 72
Amos 79, 84
Arnold 122, 166, 167, 181
Atonement of George Fox, The 144
Bachofen, Johann J 157
Barhuvad (Bareheaded) 2, 89, 174
Barnett, Samuel Augustus 87
Bataille, Georges 180
Befriaren (The Liberator) 66, 136
Bendixson, Artur 20, 21, 25, 32
Bergman, Hugo 176
Bergson, Henri 62, 63, 127
Beskow, Natanael 60, 70, 87
Birgitta (Saint) 67, 79, 92, 98–100, 128
Birgitta 92, 94, 95, 98
Bortom Birgitta (Beyond Birgitta) 163, 164, 168
Bjerre, Poul Cedergren 127, 156
Bjorck, Staffan 133
Blake, William 30
Bobrikov, Nikolai 24
Borelius, Hilma 93
Borelius, Jacob 93
Boström, Christopher Jacob 18
Bremer, Fredrika 18, 37, 76, 144
Brinton, Anna 159
Brinton, Howard 159
Buber, Martin 167, 170, 183
Catherine of Siena (Saint) 66

Chardin, Teilhard de 179
Cromwell, Oliver 141
Dante Alighieri 3, 75, 81, 108, 112, 125, 137
Darwin, Charles 19, 30
Den allra vanligaste människan (The most Ordinary Human Being) 148
Derkert, Siri 182
Drömtydaren (The Dream Interpreter) 155
Eckhart, 'Meister' 176
Feuerbach, Ludwig 11, 19
Fogelklou,
    Agnes 117
    Hans Birger (Bie) 2, 17, 117
    Ernst 2, 17
    Gertrude (Gert) 3, 12, 13, 96, 120
    Johan 2, 9, 17, 50, 75, 76, 80
    Johanna (Nan) 2, 17, 58, 107, 148
    Josefina (Fej) 2, 17, 50, 90, 106, 107, 113
    Maria (EF's mother) 2, 9, 11, 12, 17, 80, 81, 96, 106, 107
Förkunnare (Preachers) 38, 83
Form och strålning (Form and Radiance) 1, 16, 156, 177, 179, 181
Fox, George 141–144
Fox, Marion 77, 155
Fra Angelico 66, 136
Francis of Assisi (Saint) 41, 49, 50, 67, 79, 122

INDEX 205

Från hövdingen till den törnekrönte (*From Chieftain to the Crown of Thorns*) 84
Från längtansvägarna (*From the Paths of Longing*) 85
Från själens vägar (*From the Paths of the Spirit*) 86, 104, 105
Frans av Assisi (Francis of Assisi) 49, 50
Freud, Sigmund 127
Gandhi, M. K. (Mahatma) 145, 174
Gomer 34
Hägerström, Axel 30, 31, 38, 126
Hague Women's Peace Conference 75, 76
Hamilton, Florrie 168, 169
Helgon och häxor (*Saints and Witches*) 177, 178
Hitler, Adolf 150, 165
Högfors 168, 169, 173
Hosea 34
Hügel, Friedrich von 41, 42, 106, 117, 126
IAL, International Work Camps 165, 168
James, William 64, 104, 105
Jeremiah 21, 56
Jesus 24, 35, 45, 59, 64, 85, 94
Job 56, 61
Johanson, Klara 61, 70, 82, 103, 107, 117, 130, 131, 162, 169
Jones, Rufus 161
Kalmar 91, 92, 94–96, 107
Key, Ellen 20–22, 36, 91
Kierkegaard, Søren 170
Kollwitz, Käthe 36

Kreuger, Ivar 150
Kristianstad 10, 38, 44, 51, 54, 57, 60, 71, 129
Kväkaren James Nayler (*James Nayler, The Rebel Saint*) 138, 140, 141, 143
Lagerlöf, Selma 18, 19, 91, 163
Landquist, John 36
Larson, Margareta 183, 184
Larsson, Hans 64, 78, 79, 105, 148
Legender från Sveriges medeltid (*Legends from the Swedish Middle Ages*) 86
Liedholm, Johannes 90
Liedholm, Rickard 'Titten' 90, 113
Linder, Erik Hjalmar 176, 181
Linderholm, Emanuel 102
Ljus finns ändå (*There is Light Still*) 173
Lönborg, Sven 24, 25, 127
Luther, Martin 80, 124, 128
Macmurray, John 152
Malthus, Thomas 11
Maynard, Mabel 139
Medan gräset gror (*While the Grass Grows*) 21, 30, 41, 54, 67, 69, 71, 132, 175, 185
Michelsen, Ellen 111
Minnesbilder och ärenden (*Memories and messages*) 177, 179
Mussolini, Benito 116, 137
Nayler, James 138, 140, 142–144, 151, 152
Nietzsche, Friedrich 36
Nike of Samothrace 61
Norlind, Arnold 75, 97–112, 114–126, 133–40, 145, 147
Olaus Petri Society 57
Oljelund, Ivan 89

Parker, Emily 159
Pauli, Ebba 60, 87
Pendle Hill, Quaker college 159
Penn, William 151, 152
Penn, William 152
Protestant och katolik (Protestant and Catholic) 100, 101
Puvis de Chavannes 9
Resfärdig (Ready to Go) 177, 180, 181
Rilke, Rainer Maria 22
Rodin, Auguste 61
Söderblom, Nathan 21, 22, 24, 28, 29, 30, 38, 41, 47, 104
Sonntag, Wolfgang 165
Spinoza, Baruch 42
Steere, Douglas 159, 168, 172, 173
Stein, Gertrude 61
Stolpe, Sven 66
Strindberg, Per 36
Sundberg, Per 172, 173
Tagore, Rabindranath 145
Tamm, Elisabeth (Lisse) 118, 119, 154, 169
Teilhard de Chardin, Pierre 179
Thorvall, Dagny (Tove) 44, 87, 89, 151
Toynbee Hall 87
Ur fromhetslivets svensk-historia (The History of Spiritual Life in Sweden) 85
Vanås Gallery 15
Västerås 171
Vila och arbete (Leisure and Work) 129
Wägner, Elin 77, 130, 131, 143, 157, 163, 164, 169, 173, 175

Wahlström, Lydia 99
Weil, Simone 178
Weininger, Otto 35–38, 71
Whitman, Walt 21, 40, 45, 68, 111
Wilder, Thornton 138, 146
Woodbrooke Quaker College 150, 151
Woolman, John 159